EVERGLADES WILDLIFE BARONS

THE LEGENDARY PIPER BROTHERS AND THEIR WONDER GARDENS

by Charles LeBuff

RALPH CURTIS PUBLISHING

A progression of brochures in the author's collection from Everglades Wonder Gardens.
Left to right, 1942, 1956, 2005.

Printed in the United States of America

Published by:

    Ralph Curtis Publishing, Inc.
    Post Office Box 349
    Sanibel, Florida 33957
    U.S.A.

First Edition, May 2010

ISBN-10 0-88359-064-6
ISBN-13 978-0-88359-064-5

THE COVER: The original black and white cover photo from 1948 was provided through the courtesy of Anna Piper Mackereth. Her father, Bill Piper (left) and her uncle, his brother Lester, flank Tom, the Florida black bear that played the part of "Old Slewfoot" in the 1946 movie, *The Yearling*. This image was digitally colorized for use on the cover by Warren Boutchia.

Cover design by Charles LeBuff. The red and white frame around the photograph replicates the Everglades Wonder Gardens road signs which once lined the Tamiami Trail.

OTHER BOOKS BY THE AUTHOR

— *THE LOGGERHEAD TURTLE in the Eastern Gulf of Mexico*, 1990. A semi technical book on the biology and conservation of the threatened loggerhead turtle.

— *SANYBEL LIGHT*: An Historical Autobiography, 1998. A human and natural history of Sanibel Island, Florida, its lighthouse, and the J.N. "Ding" Darling National Wildlife Refuge.

— *THE CALUSAN*, 2004. An epic novel based on Florida history, featuring the 1521 death of Ponce de León at the hands of the Calusa Indians.

*   *   *   *   *

Additional copies of

EVERGLADES WILDLIFE BARONS

are available from:

Ralph Curtis Publishing
Post Office Box 349
Sanibel, Florida 33957
www.ralphcurtisbooks.com

Amber Publishing
14040 Eagle Ridge Lakes Drive
Apartment 101
Fort Myers, Florida 33912
www.sanybel.com

THE FOLLOWING TITLES ARE AVAILABLE FROM RALPH CURTIS PUBLISHING:

LIVING DRAGONS: A Natural History of the World's Monitor Lizards, by Rodney Steel.

FIELD GUIDE TO THE SNAKES AND OTHER REPTILES OF SOUTHERN AFRICA, by Bill Branch.

A FIELD GUIDE TO FROGS OF AUSTRALIA: From Port Augusta to Fraser Island, including Tasmania, by Martyn Robinson.

A FIELD GUIDE TO THE MAMMALS OF SOUTHERN AFRICA, 3rd Edition (2001), by Chris & Tilde Stuart.

A FIELD GUIDE TO THE LARGER MAMMALS OF AFRICA, by Chris & Tilde Stuart.

ADVENTURES OF A CAROLINA SNAKE HUNTER: Tales of Tails, by Heyward Clamp, Jr.

PHOTOGRAPHIC GUIDE TO BIRDS OF PERU, by Clive Byers (2007).

CONTENTS

For the people of Bonita Springs, the people of Southwest Florida, and Americans everywhere who never had a chance to meet, or who may know absolutely nothing about two of the region's most unique, dedicated, successful, and respected citizens; the bootlegging brothers, Bill and Lester Piper. They became national legends as they walked the planet during the 20th Century. They were genuine men's men who in their day were truly the undisputed barons of the wildlife world in Florida.

Preface

IN 2004, SOME FRIENDS AND I came up with a vague concept during a conversation about developing an historical website to celebrate and honor the lives of two of the most colorful entrepreneurs in the history of Southwest Florida. During our youth most of us were employees of the unique Piper brothers partnership. Wilford (Bill) and Lester Piper were the founders, owners, and operators of Everglades Wonder Gardens in Bonita Springs, Florida. This Florida wildlife attraction opened in 1937, and as I write these words it remains open and is still owned and managed by a descendant of one of the Piper brothers. Through the years my friends and I have kept in touch, and in later life, the more adventurous of us began getting together on an annual schedule. Together we would take road trips that lasted several days as we traveled through Florida to visit different points of historical interest; zoological parks, public aquariums, flea markets, and pawn shops. It was male bonding at its best.

During our forays it was inevitable that by the end of each day our conversations would come around to our memorable adventures with the brothers, Bill and Lester Piper. These were special men, and as one of the webpage contributors George Weymouth later put it, "They were as tough and powerful as Mountain Men (in a mountainless land) . . . they were Mountain Men of the Everglades." In its heyday their establishment, Everglades Wonder Gardens, was the premier wildlife exhibit in Florida. Each of us were connected to one another through these men, and any success that any of us ever made in our lives was because of the ethic of hard work that we had learned as young adults from the Pipers.

I took our discussion seriously and invited, then prodded, each of my compatriots to contribute to this project some written memories of their time at Everglades Wonder Gardens. Others, who were not tightly associated with our core group, but who had been employees during the same decade, the 1950s, were invited to contribute photographs and personal anecdotes about their life at Everglades Wonder Gardens. Most of the men that I tracked down and contacted were eager to participate, but others opted not to respond, so their reflections are not represented on my web page and their memories were lost because one or two have since passed on. Foremost, we wanted to share our youthful experiences and I wanted to gather and include some basic information about the interesting lives led by Bill and Lester. I launched the Everglades Wonder Gardens website as a link to my existing Home Page at www.sanybel.com on July 4, 2004.

I met most of the Piper family of Bonita Springs in November, 1952. Much of what I write about in this book is based on my personal knowledge and experiences, but there were aspects about Bill and Lester Piper's private lives that were unfamiliar to me. I heard just bits and pieces about their times from others, some of whom were their employees and their friends, others their enemies. In order to gather the information required for this book I had to research early twentieth century history and interview the few living individuals that were privy to both the Piper's early and later days. Time is fleeting and all concerned, including me, are running out of time.

As the concept for this book evolved, when the format graduated from my initial web page to the print media, I made the decision that its content would only cover the Piper brothers and nothing on the extended Piper family would be included beyond the brother's antecedent genealogy. I hoped to effectively end this biography with the passing of their generation — because this book, and the web page from which it has evolved, are just about the two of them. In no way did I wish to circumvent the personal privacy barriers of any living member of the Piper family. In those chapters where events are inextricably related to the biographical themes in this text, and may in some small way pertain to individuals from the younger generations of the Bonita Springs Piper family, my sources were archived public documents and are not based entirely on "one on one" dialog as a result of personal interviews with younger family members. In no instance have I ventured to assume or interpret anything other than what I discovered in those publicly available documents.

The fascinating story of the never dull lives of Bill and Lester Piper, two of America's most extraordinary men, deserves to be told. In the following pages I have made an effort to do so and bring their unique story to you. I hope you enjoy their adventurous tale.

— Charles LeBuff
Fort Myers, Florida
March 25, 2010

Acknowledgments

THE FOLLOWING PEOPLE HAVE been indispensable in enabling the idea for this book to reach fruition. My wife, Jean LeBuff, gave me the space I needed to concentrate on this book and tolerated my often bad attitude toward other important things that needed my attention. She assisted with much of the tedious research and spent hours gazing at whirring microfilm projectors as we searched for particulars to document long-forgotten events in the lives of Bill and Lester Piper. She was also a sympathetic sounding board as my writing evolved. Anna May (née Piper) Mackereth, daughter of Bill and Emie Piper, made her father's collection of papers and photographs available for my review and use and she shared details of her dad's later life with me. I so appreciate her interest in this project and all of her help and kindnesses. David Thomas Piper, Sr., son of Lester and Lucille Piper, spent hours with me talking about his memories of his parents, his uncle Bill, and Everglades Wonder Gardens. Sualyce Piper (née Littrell) Kasper, who like David and Anna is also a direct descendant of Joseph David Piper, provided me with a bonanza of genealogical information with which I could fill in many blanks about their family history. Susie's input guided me to various sources of obscure facts about the Piper family line. Charlotte Barnes, granddaughter of Ray Barnes, furnished me with biographical information about her late grandfather, in particular his tour of duty in Bonita Springs where he served as a Florida Wildlife Officer in the fifties. Ken Morrison, an employee at Everglades Wonder Gardens between 1969 and 1976, was as close to Lester Piper as anyone could ever get. The contributions Ken made to this book are exemplary. Without his input my efforts to fully portray the lives of the Piper brothers in words would have been incomplete. The noted Southwest Florida herpetologist, Tom Crutchfield, shared a few of his fondest memories with me about some of his interactions with his friend, Lester Piper. Alfred Trew and his kid brother Donald, assisted me immeasurably in putting together a timeline of the Piper brother's early years in Bonita Springs. Alfred was the first guide at Bonita Springs Reptile Gardens. This was the same post that I would fill twice during the years 1953 to 1959, after the operation was renamed Everglades Wonder Gardens. Donald Trew grew up at the Gardens, and in his youth he walked around in Bill Piper's shadow. He was Bill's nearly constant tag-along companion and sometimes even his alibi. Southwest Florida historian Alvin Lederer generously searched the archives at Rollins College, in Winter Park, Florida, to locate obscure publications that helped me tie-up some loose ends. Kathleen Zocki of Sanibel Island kindly read the final draft of my manuscript and made important editorial suggestions. Katie Heisinger of Fort Myers carefully proofread and corrected the pre-press print ready text.

Richard Beatty, Warren Boutchia, Ralph Curtis, Laban LeBuff, Dennis Morgan, and George Weymouth helped to make the timely evolution of this book possible. We all worked for the Piper brothers in the special decade of the fifties, in an era before the region's decline — before Southwest Florida was ruined by developers and crushed by an ever-expanding human population. It was at a point in time when the operation of Everglades Wonder Gardens was at its peak in botanical attractiveness, the exhibition of native wildlife, and visitor volume. At the same time, the fascinating Piper brothers were in their prime.

I owe a debt of gratitude to all who helped me, but most of all, on behalf of all my friends who were associated with Everglades Wonder Gardens and my former coworkers there, I thank Bill and Lester Piper for the knowledge and life-long skills we all inherited from them, and in particular for these two men's men having given me the pleasure of their company for but a short time, now so many years ago.

— Charles LeBuff

Introduction

HUMANS HAVE AN INTERESTING way of looking at things. Naturally, we have a way to explain ourselves in every situation. How many times have you heard someone say, "A man can't pick or choose which family he's born into"? Well, God was smiling on me because I was born into the Piper family. This book will pull you into a family that has struggled and triumphed. Impossible odds become a reality. Enough hate, love, romance, and adventure exist to fill volumes of best sellers — story after story about normal people who became legends, at least in our part of the world — women who had to be tough and men who loved but really didn't know how to show it — characters emboldened with gifts only given to a few. Who among you would stand toe to toe with a black bear, dig into an alligator cave, or try to resuscitate a lion using mouth to mouth? "No way," you might say; "that's crazy!" Well, it takes a different kind of person to walk the walk of the Pipers. Take a stroll through the lives of Lester and Bill Piper; two brothers with an interesting perspective on life. They preferred the company of animals, because animals were more trustworthy and loyal than their fellow man. Eventually, the two spoke the language of Nature and created a unique connection to the animal world. This was accomplished by providing a refuge for injured wildlife and then educating visitors about inhabitants of the vast and silent Everglades. Welcome to the world of Everglades Wonder Gardens!

> — David T. Piper, Jr., Owner of the
> Everglades Wonder Gardens
> Son of David Piper, Sr.
> Grandson of Lester Piper
> Great nephew of Bill Piper

Wilford James Piper, born January 8, 1900, in Lancaster, Fairfield County, Ohio.

Lester Thomas Piper, born December 13, 1902, in Lancaster, Fairfield County, Ohio.

Chapter 1

Dangerous Times

DETROIT WAS HEATING UP . . . no, better put, it was becoming bloody hot! The city's murder thermometer hadn't quite yet reached the bloodbath point, like nearby Chicago's did during the infamous "Saint Valentine's Day Massacre" of February 14, 1929, but Michigan's "Motor City" wasn't lagging too far behind the "Windy City." By 1930, either Detroit or its downriver neighboring city of Wyandotte, Michigan, was poised to attain the leadership level in Midwestern America's era of bloody, deadly violence. It seemed that these Michigan cities were trying to outshoot each other.

The great American social experiment known as Prohibition was created by ratification of the Eighteenth Amendment of the Constitution of the United State of America, on January 16, 1919, but the Michigan Legislature had seen to it that Detroit and the rest of the state was dry a year earlier. Nation-wide prohibition was launched October 28, 1919, with Congressional passage of the Volstead Act. This Act enabled the United States to enforce the provisions of the Eighteenth Amendment, which was formally known as the National Prohibition Act. President Woodrow Wilson promptly vetoed this enabling Act because of the technical conflicts he saw with acceptable wartime use of alcohol.

On the same day of his veto, the anti-alcohol Congress, driven by the recent ratification of the amendment by thirty-six states, overrode President Wilson's action and the Act became law. The text of the Eighteenth Amendment reads:

Section 1. After one year from the ratification of this article the manufacture, sale, or transportation of intoxicating liquors within, the importation thereof into, or the exportation thereof from the United States and all territory subject to the jurisdiction thereof for beverage purposes is hereby prohibited.

Section 2. The Congress and the several States shall have concurrent power to enforce this article by appropriate legislation.

Section 3. This article shall be inoperative unless it shall have been ratified as an amendment to the Constitution by the legislatures of the several States, as provided in the Constitution, within seven years from the date of the submission hereof to the States by the Congress.

*   *   *   *   *

Harry Bernstein was a hard-working Polish Jew who had immigrated to New York City late in the nineteenth century. In 1902, he relocated his wife and seven children to Detroit, Michigan, where they opened a shoe repair business in the industrial center of the city. The eldest son, Abe, had been born circa 1892 and had spent his formative years on the streets of New York. By the time he reached nine years of age, he was a smart-ass and street tough kid. Then he and his siblings were uprooted and translocated to the Jewish ghetto of Detroit. Young Abe was already criminally incorrigible. Times were tough in the fast-growing, fast-paced city, and opportunities were few for inner-city youngsters of all ethnic backgrounds during this era. New educational opportunities awaited the Bernstein kids on the soot-covered streets in the bowels of industrialized Detroit. By this time three other Bernstein sons were out of control, and like their older brother they too grew up unsupervised to roam the mean streets of Detroit. They emulated and envied Abe, and instead of being educated in a formal school classroom, they received a crime-ridden street sense that followed most of them throughout their lives. As adolescents, they envied the flashy-dressed two-bit gangsters that were part of their community. These were the men who drove luxury automobiles and were attired in the most stylish of clothing and flashed bankrolls that would choke a horse as they plied their trades. When Michigan politicians declared the state dry in 1918, it's estimated there were 1,500 legitimate saloons and 800 unlicensed blind pigs[1] in the city of Detroit. The latter establishments were ordinary speakeasies and similarly were customarily controlled by organized crime figures. If criminals didn't own them outright by the time the Bernstein boys were in their early twenties the owners were strong-armed into paying demanded kickbacks.

Several gangs of youthful thugs had evolved in the underworld of the city with Abe Bernstein at the helm. In Detroit many shady characters who were connected to a criminal faction usually owned blind pigs. Many of these crooks also maneuvered into trade unions, particularly the Cleaners and Dyers Union of Detroit, where their extortion practices wreaked havoc in that industry. The Bernsteins, and their group of criminal associates, fit into a laundry list of criminal activity. You name it; they were participants. They were gamblers, extortionists, pimps, highjackers, and bootleggers. The gang members were inextricably involved in any other illegal pursuit imaginable. Such was their means of meeting their organizational needs and maintaining their high profile life style.

Since adolescence the Bernstein boys were completely out of parental control and had made hard choices as they began to associate with a core of petty hoodlums in their neighborhood who at first called themselves the "Boys." Over time the boys somehow acquired their own identity and became known as the "Purple Gang." The exact origins of this name are unknown but for most of the first half of the twentieth century their criminal activities would exact a toll from the livelihoods of Detroit's workers and the heart of the city's business community.

The rein of the Purples was launched on May 1, 1918, when the 1916 enactment of the Michigan State Prohibition Referendum took effect. Prohibition gave gangsters across America a new lease on life, and illegal opportunities galore. From this quirk in America's history was born a bonanza of new rackets for the

Purples and their ilk to invent and control. The Purple Gang would graduate to higher levels of misdeeds because of Prohibition. Abe Bernstein would become a mentor for the young criminals following in his footsteps. The gang aligned themselves early on with an older group known in gangster circles as the Oakland Sugar House Gang. This union was strategic because the Purples thought they would attain the respect of competing underworld figures through this association. By 1923, the Purples had absorbed the Oakland Sugar House Gang and they became consolidated. Shootings and murders had become a regular part of their repertoire as they consolidated their power and influence. Their dastardly influence expanded and their loose-knit gang association was strengthened through these violent acts.

By the late twenties the Purple Gang had divided into separate entities, each responsible for their own criminal interests. Gang members worked the many extortion opportunities in the city. Some ran slick bookmaking enterprises. Some began operating lucrative blind pigs. Others were imbedded in the illegal alcohol importation and sales industry. One branch began a bevy of gambling enterprises, while others concentrated on high-jacking illegal alcohol. Still others expanded into stealing and cracking safes from the many successful businesses in the Detroit area. One other notable faction branched out into the lucrative field of kidnapping, and authorities didn't overlook this during their investigation into the sad Lindbergh kidnapping case. Members of the Purple Gang were among the first to be suspected and brought in for questioning by police detectives who were investigating this heinous crime.

One of Detroit's premier bookmakers was Sam Solomon. It was his brainstorm that led to the organization of a new enterprise in the Purple Gang's operational forte. One of the Purple Gang's most lucrative enterprises was Solomon's creation of the "Little Jewish Navy." This consisted of a small fleet of privately owned speedboats that would ply the Detroit River and high-jack liquor that was being transported by bootleggers from Canada to the United States by other gangs. The crews of the Little Jewish Navy were very successful in their piracy, but distribution of the goods became a problem. This forced association with other criminal elements and the influence of the Purples grew outside of Detroit. Growth produced personnel problems and since the Purple Gang was always a loose confederation of bad guys its growth sometimes cost lives. The first indication that growth was being taken seriously came to light in March of 1927. Startled residents of Detroit's Milaflores Apartments sprang out of bed when their sleep ended shortly after 4:30 in the morning. They were awakened to the sound of automatic weapons being discharged in their building. After the shooting stopped, three victims were discovered inside the entry of Apartment 308. Two of them had been shot dead; their bodies riddled with machine gun bullets. The third man was barely alive and would die later, but not before he gave police a considerable amount of detail about the assailants. By pulling off these violent gangland murders the Purple Gang had reached the notoriety of the big time. The Purple Gang of Detroit was certainly operating on a renewed violent track that if left unchecked by authorities could surpass the bloodletting of the Chicago mob.

By the end of the decade, the Purples were invited to travel to New York City to attend a conference that had been called by the hierarchy of the New York mobsters. These were men who were on their way to crime superstardom — Luciano, Lansky, and Torrio among them. Earlier, Torrio had graced Al Capone with the leadership in Chicago, and Capone was present at the New York conference. The group carefully planned the organization of a national monopoly that would control the illicit booze industry in the United States. Monies made during Prohibition would later be invested in distilleries and breweries if, and when, consumption of alcohol became legal again. They were all criminally intelligent men and thought their brainstorming session would guarantee a comfortable future for themselves should their lucrative outlaw enterprises dry up one day.

Al Capone watched from Chicago as illegal booze profits skyrocketed in Detroit and the downriver communities in the late twenties. By the end of the decade, profits in Detroit would surpass $215 million. Al Capone went to Michigan, trying to get a piece of the action, but soon left after being told, "That is our river." by Abe

Bernstein and the Purple Gang. But, at the end of the discussion he had succeeded in adding the Purples to his syndicate's cadre of suppliers of Canadian whiskey.

With the impetus brought on by a significantly increased cash flow, the Purple Gang became more brazen and its representatives soon controlled, or were receiving a goodly percentage of the profits from most of the blind pig operations in Detroit. They also took control of most of the docks and boat slips along the Detroit waterfront for operations of the Little Jewish Navy. They even went so far as to demand a monetary kickback on all illegal liquor that made it across the river from Canada and reached Detroit apart from their own river operations.

In 1929, Michigan's head of prohibition enforcement issued a directive to his agency. They were to rid the city of Detroit of the Purple Gang; they were instructed to stop rumrunning on the Detroit River. This thirty-two mile long river connects Lake Saint Clair with Lake Erie. Its breadth creates an international border between the United States and Canada, and physically separates Detroit, Michigan, from Windsor, Ontario. Wyandotte is located on the river and situated about eleven miles south of Detroit. Wyandotte had the reputation of being the toughest rumrunning area in the United States.

Bootlegger Joe Tocco and his brother, Sam, ruled the bootlegging industry in Wyandotte. Their involvement with, or their allegiance to, the Purple Gang was unclear, but in order to be as successful as they were, there had to be a connection between their liquor operations and the Purples. On November 6, 1931, violence erupted in Wyandotte when three bootleggers were gunned down in a joint known as "Tears," a speakeasy on Biddle Avenue in Wyandotte. The three were rivals of the Tocco organization and their two groups had feuded for years to determine who controlled rumrunning in Wyandotte. Authorities immediately pointed fingers at the Toccos, but didn't have enough evidence to make anything stick. These killings were dubbed the Wyandotte Massacre and were responsible for Joe Tocco leaving the rackets. What pushed him to leave totally was the payback in 1932, when his expensive home in an upscale section of Wyandotte was nearly completely destroyed by a bomb. After these eye-opening episodes, bootleggers began to look around for other ways to make a living and those that had been frugal and saved their money would soon reach out and seek new enterprises and change their lifestyle to save their lives and those of their families. But, it didn't happen until a few others paid their dues for their financial success — and in a big-time deadly way.

In April 1930, two Ohio-born brothers with the German-rooted surname of Piper lived with their young wives in Wyandotte, Michigan. The men had been residents of the city since 1921. Their homes were relatively expensive for the period and a canal connected their properties to the Detroit River. Wilford "Bill" and Frances Piper lived at 53 Orange Street, and Lester and Lucille Piper beside them, at 59 Orange, in the Yachtman's Home Subdivision. A boathouse was located on Lester's canal front, thus his property was valued more than his brother Bill's on the Wayne County tax rolls. Ironically, their residences were located less than a mile from the Wyandotte Police Station. Bill, the elder brother, had taken up the bootlegging trade after being discharged from the U.S. Navy. By 1930, and by criminal standards, the brothers had been very successful financially; exceptionally so for men of such young age. However, by this time in their lives they had also matured enough to realize that deadly violence was becoming pervasive among their cohorts. The aggressiveness of their competitors would soon strike very close to home, and ultimately change their lives. Only after one of them experienced the fury would they be convinced that it was time to end this highly rewarding criminal career and get out of the business — retreat from the lifestyle while the getting out was good, and at a time when their cash reserves were substantial.

The Piper brothers' outlook on life and their future involvement in the bootlegging trade changed suddenly when Bill was gunned down and left seriously wounded by some of their competition. He and a few of his personal cohorts were blindsided — attacked unexpectedly by members of a rival rumrunning gang. Their adversaries came out of nowhere with their weapons blazing. In the melee, Bill took a round to the upper left chest before the attackers were driven off by return gunfire. Miraculously, despite the life-threatening bullet hole, Bill Piper survived this wound. In later years, when he often toiled without a shirt in the Florida sun, the scar would be on display for all to see[2]. New acquaintances who became close to him in a work environment eventually got around to asking him about it. Bill would relive the close call the bullet scar represented, but he wouldn't often tell anyone why it happened. Lead slugs would pierce Bill Piper's body again many years later, and bring him, once again, dangerously close to the brink of death.

Before this deadly encounter, the Piper boys had operated with their own circle of trusted people, a small gang if you will, and were able to remain free agents in this very profitable enterprise on the Detroit River. The brothers had always used good judgment, were diplomatic in their association with fellow rumrunners, and up until this assassination attempt had managed to survive the infighting that was so common among their greedy rivals. They had earlier managed to elude a take-over, that would have ended up with them being completely dominated by Detroit's Purple Gang. The Purple Gang's Little Jewish Navy would occasionally arrange for the Piper brothers' speedy motor vessel, the forty-two-foot *Neptune,* to move whiskey from Canada across the Detroit River to the alcohol-thirsty United States. The Pipers managed to maintain reasonable independence, but to survive in the business they had to be connected to the criminal network through some kind of financial arrangement with major Wyandotte bootleggers who were closely associated with the Purple Gang. Everyone who transported liquor across the Detroit River from Canada to the United States was in some way connected to them, however low key and seemingly innocuous that connection might be. Dollars had to be channeled and regularly flow between the Piper brothers and the Purples in some fashion or the young men would have been in peril from the beginning, and someone would have tried to take Bill Piper out much earlier in his criminal career. Joe Tocco was the intermediary.

Wyandotte was just far enough away from Detroit that they could enjoy their independence and hold on to most of the fruits of their labor. The Piper's operation was connected to a loose-knit band of organized independent bootleggers that some sources refer to as "The Shipyard Gang." One can assume this name was derived because of a connection of some sort with the Detroit Shipbuilding Company's Wyandotte facility. More than likely the vast, mostly abandoned waterways of the shipyard filled their needs because it sometimes offered a safe haven for their off-loading operations. Someone they knew through their connections, possibly a relative, like a half-brother, probably helped make this happen.

With the demise of Prohibition and the nation's return to the legalization of alcohol and alcoholic beverages, Abe Bernstein and his cast of surviving cronies had been defeated. Other criminal operations that were controlled by the Purple Gang in and around Detroit were quietly transferred to the better-organized Italian Mafia. The Purple Gang was history. Abe would live out his years in Miami, affiliated with a number of syndicate-owned gambling casinos. He died on March 7, 1968. The Piper brothers had gone straight before Prohibition ended and were poised to go on to much better, but not necessarily safer, things.

Chapter 2

Family Roots

JOHANN FREDERIC PFEIFFER, THE ANTECEDENT of the Piper family that is germane to this book, probably arrived in the United States in the late 1820s. He was born on February 28, 1804, in Europe in the Kingdom of Hannover. This area became a province of Prussia, in 1866. After national unification in 1971, it is now a major city in the Northern German state of Lower Saxony. By 1830, the young immigrant had settled in Lancaster, Ohio. During this period, this region of Ohio was being populated by a substantial number of Germanic immigrants. As many newly arrived Europeans did, he Americanized his name. He became Joseph Frederick Piper. He usually went by his middle name, and this practice would become commonplace in the future among males in the Piper family. Frederick continued his trade as a cooper, a manufacturer of wooden stave barrels, and he also dabbled in real estate and bought and sold property in and around Lancaster. In 1834, he married Mary Ann Wald who would bear twelve children. They settled into life in a cabin on Stony Hill Road, near Hamburg, Ohio. J. Frederick Piper died on July 12, 1886, at the age of eighty-two, two years after the couple had celebrated fifty years of marriage. Ann survived her husband by almost six years and passed away on January 9, 1893. The couple is buried in the Wald family plot in Saint Mary Catholic Cemetery in Lancaster, Ohio.

The second of the twelve Piper children was Joseph. He was born on April 1, 1836, in Lancaster and rose to the position of Street Commissioner for that city. On Christmas Day, 1856, he married Mary Fisher and they would have eight children. Joseph passed away on August 20, 1921, in Centerville, Ohio, and his wife survived him until August 22, 1925.

According to the 1900 United States Census, Joseph Piper was living with his son Joseph (Joe) David Piper and his family, on South Broad Street, in Lancaster, on June 23, 1900. He would later move into his daughter Henrietta's home in Centerville, where he would spend his final years.

Joe Piper, the second of the eight children, was born November 1, 1858, in Lancaster, Ohio. On May 4, 1887 he married Alice Elizabeth Hankison who was born in 1859. Five children were produced from this union, but it was marred by what would become a series of tragedies, which when put into perspective and considered as a whole, were surely the most severe in the history of this Piper family. However, future family members would face elements of traumatic tragedy and loss, too. First, Alice took ill and died on September 28, 1894, during a diphtheria and scarlet fever epidemic that swept across Ohio. Alice and Joe's first-born, Joseph David Piper, Jr., who came into this world on May 20, 1888, also died of scarlet fever, in 1897. The second child, John, was born on November 30, 1889, and contacted scarlet fever but recovered, only to be infected by tuberculosis. He was sent to an Oklahoma ranch/sanitarium to recover. He did recover, and later married Hortence Freefau who bore him one son, James Piper. John Piper and his small family relocated to Detroit, Michigan. The third child of Joe and Alice Piper was Alice Ethel Piper who was born on September 14, 1891, but sadly, she too, succumbed to scarlet fever on October 18, 1893. Their fourth child was Ruth Perea Piper who was born on January 16, 1893, and married Frank James Page on May 9, 1914. She passed away in January, 1971. The last Piper child from this union was Johanna Edith Piper, who was born on August 16, 1894, survived childhood, and died June 29, 1989.

During this sad time Joe Piper served as a police officer with the Lancaster Police Department. According to the current Lancaster Chief of Police, David Bailey, Joe Piper was employed by that agency from January 1890 to January 1901, and his official photograph is yet housed in the police station, but his personnel folder no longer exists. There is some anecdotal evidence in his known employment history which indicates that following his tour of duty with the Lancaster Police Department, Joe Piper went to work for the Lancaster Fire Department for a few years[3].

Joe Piper had another burden to bear, and he carried it to the end of his life. Amid an occasional bout of depression, he would often relive the story with family and confidants. Sometime during his law enforcement career he apprehended and arrested a horse thief in the notorious Lancaster hop-yards. This was a neighborhood in the city's East End and it was rife with thieves, saloons, brothels, and associated criminal activity. Police officers spent a considerable amount of time fighting crime in this recently annexed area of the city. While he was walking his prisoner to the Police Station, the man begged to be released from his handcuffs just long enough to relieve himself. Officer Piper obliged him, but with his hands free the man decided to make a break for it and dashed away. Joe ordered him to stop, then drew his pistol. He fired a round that was intended to pass over the man's head, but his aim was off and the bullet struck the fleeing felon and fatally wounded him. Joseph D. Piper could never shake the memory.

On November 4, 1896, Joe remarried. His second wife was Ohio native Anna May Magdalene Messbarger, who was about twenty-one years his junior. Their first child was James Wilford Piper who was born on January 8, 1900. A second son followed on December 13, 1902, and was named Thomas Lester Piper. A daughter, Anna Mae Piper was born on May 24, 1905, and her birth would complete Anna's childbearing. Years later, James and Thomas Piper would use their middle names exclusively and they would be known as Wilford and Lester, respectively, for the rest of their lives. Wilford always preferred to be known as Bill, and his closest associates would call Lester, Les. Their given names appear on their birth records and they also appear so-named on the Enumerator's Sheet recorded in the U.S. Census on February 2,

1920, for Lancaster, Fairfield County, Ohio. However, on all of the deeds and other legal documents they would execute in Florida, and there were many, the brothers always signed their names as Wilford J. Piper[4] and Lester T. Piper. At the time of his Naval enlistment, Bill is Wilford James Piper.

The Piper family, circa 1911, in Lancaster, Ohio. Left to right — Anna Mae Piper, Anna May Magdalene (née Messbarger) Piper, Wilford James Piper, Joseph David Piper, and Lester Thomas Piper.

By 1921, the year of his father's death, the Joseph D. Piper family moved from Lancaster, Ohio, to Florida for a few years and then on to Wyandotte, Michigan. Before leaving Lancaster, Joe left his two surviving daughters from his first marriage with their uncle, James Hankison, a brother of their mother. James would raise Ruth and Edith and bequeath them his money and property when he died. Joseph David Piper was affectionately known as "Dode" by his progeny, and for a time after his retirement he worked as a guard for the Detroit Shipbuilding Company, at one time the largest shipbuilding operation in the Great Lakes region. The company had one yard in Detroit and another in Wyandotte. The latter operation shut down in 1920 to curtail rising costs of operation. No longer maintained, the wharves, piers, waterways, and structures of the once thriving facility fell into disrepair. Shipbuilding had declined after World War I ended, and the company would cease operations altogether in 1929.

In the early thirties Joe and Anna were caring for their daughter Anna Mae's two girls, June and Crystal, who were living under their grandparents' roof in Wyandotte, Michigan. In those years the family was listed in the various Wyandotte City Directories, and Joe's occupation was simply listed as a laborer. Joe Piper would continue to travel to Florida to escape the cold Michigan winters and visit his sons, Bill and Lester, until ailments associated with old age forced him to stop traveling. On his way back home in the spring, he continued to always stop and visit with his daughters in Ohio, dividing his time between Ruth and Edith.

Following his death on August 22, 1944, Joe Piper was interred with his first spouse, Alice, in the Saint Mary Catholic Cemetery in Lancaster, Ohio. In 1945, his widow, Anna, would relocate to Florida to be with her children.

Chapter 3

Growing Up

CHILD LABOR LAWS WERE nonexistent at the beginning of the twentieth century and it was a time of life when things were not exactly easy for Joe Piper and his second family. Bill and Lester Piper were in the same boat as other children of the times. If a family unit needed additional funds to survive, the kids went to work to help out. The Piper boys were enrolled in a Lancaster parochial school and neither was an exemplary student. They found themselves in almost daily conflict with the nuns, and thus frequently subjected to painful corporal punishment because of their constant mischievous misbehavior. This abuse resulted in their lack of interest and so, somewhat justifiably, their vigor for an education waned at an early age. For one of them, school ended at a very early age.

From all accounts it appears that Bill Piper never completed high school[5]. According to his son, David, Lester always said that he had had enough abuse and gave up on his education by the end of the third grade and joined the workforce. He said he just got fed up with being constantly disciplined by being struck on his knuckles with a wooden paddle by the nuns. Bill, who aspired to see the broader world beyond Lancaster, Ohio, enlisted in the U.S. Naval Reserve and went on active duty at eighteen years, four months of age. Earlier, he had lied about his age and was admitted to the Navy Coast Defense Reserve, in 1916. Lester would find work in construction and become a pipe fitter. He was in his very late teens when the family made the move to Michigan. There, like many other young workers, he would hire on in the automotive industry. His automobile career, with the Dodge plant in Detroit, wouldn't last long once big brother Bill finally got home from his second naval enlistment. Their older half-brother, John, once he had recovered from his bout with tuberculosis, had relocated to Detroit. He later married and went to work for the Chrysler Corporation. John passed away in the early thirties and left one son, James, who graduated from the Chrysler Institute with a degree in tool design, in 1947.

In their youth the Piper boys were typical rambunctious youngsters. They loved being outside to explore their surroundings. The brothers fished every nearby pond, lake, creek, or river — when they weren't chasing every snake and turtle they saw during those days afield. They soon had a collection of local species from around the Lancaster, Ohio, area and after their relocation to Michigan their keen interest in a variety of living things continued to grow.

When Joe's children were young preteens, the Piper family left Lancaster and migrated to the Sunshine State where they lived for a few years. They spent about a year in Dade County, in the Miami area, but then settled in Largo on the Gulf Coast. Life in Florida was not a family vacation where everyone soaked up the Florida sunshine and played. Everyone worked. Joe had truck farmed in Ohio earlier in his life. In 1900, his occupation on the U.S. Census form shows that he was both on the police force and a truck farmer. He became involved in winter truck farming around Largo, although there are no records to indicate the Piper family owned property in that part of Hillsborough County. Not long before they arrived there, Largo and Saint Petersburg became part of Pinellas County when, in 1911, Hillsborough County was split and Pinellas County was established. Joe Piper either leased farmland on which to grow winter vegetables or he managed a truck farm for someone else. The Piper boys quickly fell in love with Florida. Their interest in reptiles and other wild animals blossomed further after they were exposed to the variety of wild things that Florida abundantly offered for young naturalists in those days. Years later, in an interview, Bill Piper remembered catching his first Florida snake in Largo — a venomous coral snake.

During a 1959 interview, Bill Piper said, "The farm produced well, but there was no market at the time, so we all moved over to Saint Petersburg where our father got a job on the fire department. That is what he did back in Lancaster, Ohio, where we were born."

While in Florida, Anna Piper took in laundry and labored washing and ironing to earn extra income. The children helped her whenever they were needed for chores. No job was too small. Hauling water and hanging clothes were all part of their routine. The boys would deliver the completed laundry to the customers their mother served. Bill and Lester would spend long days commercial fishing to earn extra income for the family, and sold their catch at the end of the day to help bring money into the household. While fishing they would always be on the lookout for a snake or a turtle to add to their collection. The Piper boys would offset their lack of formal education with remarkable common sense, a hard-driving work ethic, and a personal desire to attain an element of success in the long lives that they hoped lay ahead of them.

The Piper family remained in Saint Petersburg at least until the early part of 1916. When they left Florida, they relocated to Wyandotte, Michigan, where they first lived at 122 Front Street, in a home Joe and Anna Piper purchased.

Chapter 4

Anchors Aweigh

AFTER THE PIPER FAMILY relocated from Florida to Michigan, Bill Piper lied about his age, and at sixteen managed to join the U.S. Navy Coast Defense Reserve. This class of naval participation was established by a federal act on August 29, 1916, which created the Naval Reserve Force[6]. The United States eventually declared war against the Central Powers, notably Germany and the Austro-Hungarian Empire, on April 4, 1917, and Bill Piper enlisted for four years of active duty; volunteering for general service in the U.S. Naval Reserve Force on May 7, 1918, a little more than a year after our entry into World War I and a few months after his eighteenth birthday[7].

When Bill underwent his induction physical, he stood six-feet, one-inch tall. It was noted that, with the exception of a small scar on the right side of his forehead and small scars on his fingers and knees, he had no other body scars or markings. He had already received most of his basic training as an enrollee of the U.S. Navy Coast Defense Reserve. He attended an abbreviated boot camp session and shipped out from the Naval Training Center on June 12, as a Seaman, Second Class. Bill arrived in Europe on June 30, 1918. While in Europe, he was assigned to several Naval Air Stations from June 30, 1918, until January 6, 1919. These were located in Pauillac and Moutchic[8], France, and Gujan, Italy.

Photo courtesy of Anna Piper Mackereth.

Bill Piper, in 1916, after he became a member of the Naval Coast Defense Reserve, and prior to when he elected to enroll for active Naval duty, in 1918, just after the United States entered World War I. The white braid sewn into the seam on his right shoulder indicates he is a Seaman, but his class cannot be determined because the identifying wrist markings on his uniform sleeve are hidden in this photograph.

His Seaman rating was confirmed on December 18, 1918. The air stations he was assigned to were bases for airships[9]. After the Armistice was signed and hostilities ended on November 11, 1918, Bill left Europe and was reassigned stateside to the Naval

Training Camp, Pelham Bay, New York. Bill's sea duty pay, in 1919, was $38.40 per month. He was transferred to inactive duty on March 1, 1919, and thereafter he drifted to the west coast and Alaska before returning to Wyandotte, Michigan, late in 1919. Bill

Photo courtesy of Anna Piper Mackereth.

Bill Piper, circa 1919, while in an inactive duty status from the Navy. According to his notation on the backing of the frame that holds this photo, it was taken just after he had returned to Wyandotte, Michigan, from Alaska, where he had worked for a fishing season aboard a sailing vessel as a commercial salmon fisherman.

would be recalled to active duty on January 12, 1921, and he served aboard the USS *Delaware*. Prior to Naval reactivation, and according to the 1920 U.S. Census, Bill was living with his parents and siblings in Wyandotte and was employed as a night watchman in an area factory. He was in and out of active service several times.

Bill became "a trusty shellback" when he crossed the equator aboard the USS *Nevada* on January 21, 1921, during a South American good will cruise. He was awarded a certificate that recognized this achievement from the Domain of Neptunus Rex[10]. The USS *Nevada* would later make history during World War II. She had been launched in 1914, then modernized between August 1927 and January 1930, and was at Pearl Harbor on December 7, 1941, moored near the USS *Arizona*. The USS *Nevada* was the only battleship in the harbor to get underway that infamous day. Although hit by one torpedo and struck by at least six bombs, she took out several Japanese aircraft before she was beached to avoid sinking. The battleship later participated in the bombardment of German fortifications during the Normandy invasion. Later, her fourteen-inch guns would bombard Iwo Jima and Okinawa in the Pacific Theater.

On April 15, 1922, Bill Piper sent the following letter to the Commandant of the Great Lakes Naval Training Center, Ninth Naval District:

> I have had a request for recall to active duty for training for the purpose of bringing the USS *Dubuque* now at the Navy Yard at Portsmouth to Detroit.
>
> My enrollment will expire May 7, 1922 and I must have my Discharge before May 15, 1922 so that I can be reenrolled to make this cruise, and it is requested that my Discharge be forwarded to me at 358 East Larned Street, Detroit, Mich. promptly on May 7, 1922.
>
> > Wilford James Piper
> > Q.M.C3 Class
> > Home address
> > > 76 Third St.
> > > Wyandotte, Mich.

On May 4, 1922, Bill was reenrolled and rated Quartermaster, Third Class ,and committed to serve four years. Bill was promoted to Quartermaster, Second Class[11] on December 1, 1924 and was assigned to the USS *Yantic*.

Bill Piper was honorably discharged on May 2, 1926, at the rank of Quartermaster, Second Class. It is interesting that during the physical examination nearest to and prior to his release date his scars (as noted in 1918) were the same, but by the time of his transfer to inactive duty on December 19, 1922, he had added several tattoos and grew one-inch in height. He had the following tattoos: a six-point nautical star on his left shoulder, an anchor on his forearm, a rope above his wrist, and a butterfly on his right shoulder. There was no reference to any upper body scars.

Bill returned home and he would soon enlist in another reserve naval outfit. This time it would be the much better paying Little Jewish Navy.

Chapter 5

Life on the River

AFTER HIS NAVY ENLISTMENT was up in 1926, Bill Piper was lured to a career on the Detroit River — at a time when good boatmen who were unafraid of risk and who were cautious could make loads of money. Busy bootleggers were bringing so much illegal liquor into Michigan that the Canadian distilleries were actually running out of bottles and there was a shortage. Bill was offered an entry-level job to transport empties back across the Detroit River to Ontario where they would be cleaned and refilled. From today's perspective one might say that Bill Piper was a true pioneer in recycling.

According to the 1922 Wyandotte City Directory, while Bill was away from home during his active naval service, Lester continued to live with his parents and worked as a machinist's helper. By the time the 1926 Directory was published, Bill had been honorably discharged from the U.S. Naval Reserve Force and was again a civilian and living back at his parents' home. The older Pipers had moved to 17 Orange Street, in Wyandotte, and Bill was in residence with his new wife, Frances. Bill's occupation is not listed, but Lester is supposed to be a painter. By 1930, the Piper brothers had each purchased and lived in their expensive canal-front homes. That year, on the U.S. Census form, Lester is listed as a building contractor and Bill as a house painter. By Prohibition's end in 1933, Bill is no longer living in Wyandotte,[12] but Lester is still listed as a building contractor residing at his house on Orange Street. Lester and Lucille are still included in the 1936 Wyandotte City Directory as residents of 59 Orange Street and Lester's occupation is given as a carpenter contractor.

As Bill became more prosperous because of the infusion of his alcohol importation income he decided he and Lester would stop rowing skiff-loads of booze across the Detroit River and he would spring for a speedboat. Later in life Bill claimed that his speedboat was the fastest motor vessel on the Detroit River. It had to be very fast, because by some accounts the boats of rumrunners often exceeded speeds of seventy miles per hour. They were much faster watercraft than the standard thirty-five-foot patrol boats that were manufactured for the U.S. Border Patrol who usually chased them. Bill's speedboat was powered by a twelve-cylinder Continental engine and would really scat. After Bill attained a self-sufficient position in the liquor distribution system, Lester continued to work with his brother in the expanded enterprise. While working together as a team with shared crews their involvement in bootlegging grew and their profits soared.

Bill and Lester often told a story about this particular boat when they were in a talkative mood and reminiscing about their career on the Detroit River. While they and their crew were busy unloading a boatful of booze at a predetermined spot along the Wyandotte shoreline, several patrol boats swept in on them in the dark. To avoid being apprehended with the evidence, everyone jumped overboard, swam ashore, and then ran off in different directions to gain distance from the booze and the boat and the law. The officials seized the boat and cargo and towed it to a police facility elsewhere on the river. In the wee hours a few nights later, after he had ascertained where the speedboat was moored, Lester drove Bill to a destination upriver from where his boat was moored and dropped him off. Bill was determined that he was going to repossess his boat. In the dark, he cautiously walked to the edge of the river, waded in, and then proceeded to quietly float downriver and swim up to the boat. He severed all the lines that were holding the boat fast to the dock with a knife he had brought along. He then pushed the boat away from the pilings out into the river current and swam along with the speedboat, carefully guiding it to a dark location where Lester and their band of people were waiting.

Another incident, this time involving Lester's bravado, took place on the shore of the Detroit River and didn't come to light until over forty years after the fact, in 1976. I will discuss details of this in due time, in Chapter Twenty.

The *Neptune*, and her crew of bootleggers, circa 1930, moored in the Orange Street canal, in Wyandotte, Michigan.

Bill soon purchased an additional boat for their work on the river. He wanted not only speed but also a roomy vessel with the capacity to haul many more cases of whiskey and other Canadian alcoholic beverages per trip. The *Neptune* was a forty-two-foot vessel that was powered by a Diesel engine. She would haul about four hundred cases per trip, along with armed crewmembers[13], and travel at a high rate of speed. During a river crossing with a load of illegal booze, they not only had to avoid and outrun law enforcement, they also had to be ready to cope with would-be hijackers. Bill was skipper of the boat and Lester functioned as the *Neptune*'s chief engineer. Lester had to take a course in Diesel mechanics to be able to keep the boat's engine tweaked for its best performance.

Bootlegging on the Detroit River was a year-round job. Boats worked fine for crossings most of the year, but in the dead of winter, after the Detroit River had frozen solid, it was common for the more industrious among the bootleggers to use the ice as a means to make their lucrative deliveries of contraband liquor from Canada to Michigan. It was not uncommon for automobiles or light trucks that were heavily laden with booze to cross the river by driving on the ice. Countless vehicles that were over-filled with heavy cases of liquor broke through the ice and the drivers went for a swim. Some drowned, and their vehicles and cargo ended up on the river bottom. The Piper gang opted to use more labor-intensive but safer methods to get the job done in the winter and to keep the cash flowing. They manually pulled flat-bottomed scows that were loaded to the gunwales with booze across the ice of the Detroit River in the worst of weather. Lack of visibility during snowstorms gave them the best kind of cover and several crossings could be made each night during the most inclement weather. Lester and his sidekick, Art Rohmer, worked as a team and would sometimes slide four boatloads of expensive whiskey across the ice in one night. They would bundle up warmly and clamp crampons to the soles of their boots. The spikes would penetrate the ice and give them the necessary traction needed to pull their load. Then they would slip into heavy harnesses and buckle them on. A line from each of their harnesses was then tethered to the front of the boat. In unison, they would strain to get the load moving. Once the boat started to move, they literally ran across the ice for a mile or more to keep ahead of the sliding scow. When they were winded and had to take a break, they had to keep moving and let the boat coast to a stop. Otherwise, they chanced being run over by the heavy load. The money just kept sliding in.

Many years later, during a conversation with Lester about his early days in Michigan, Ken Morrison asked, "Wouldn't it have been easier to take one of those light T-Models and run it across?" Lester thought for a moment and then replied, "Hell no, then your truck and your whiskey would be on the bottom. I took a boat. In case it broke through, it'd still float!"

There is no record of how much the Piper brothers earned or what the final dollar figure was of the fortunes they amassed in their seven-year bootlegging career. When speaking with confidants, they would always claim that they made lots of money, but they would always stop short of disclosing just how much they earned when asked. It had to be very substantial if their take was up to par with their cohorts in Wyandotte. If a big-time bootlegger loaded five thousand cases of whiskey aboard his vessel in Windsor, his upfront cost would be $200,000. When he safely made the short passage and his crew unloaded the cargo in the United States, he would make a profit on the load of $725,000. Then from that, he had to pay off his crew and any officials he may have bribed to take the night off, or who were asked to work some other section of the river on a particular night. Those law enforcement officials who were in his pocket knew just where his operation would be making a crossing and they would patrol another sector of their area of responsibility. One highly successful Wyandotte bootlegger would later admit that he had made $50,000,000.00[14] in just the first two years following the enactment of Prohibition.

Although there is no documented evidence to show that the Piper brothers had a connection to Joe Tocco, they all were getting rich from the same line of work. Tocco owned a vacation home outside of Wyandotte, and one day when they were together Tocco said to Bill, "Can you find me some painters? I need to have my house up in the woods painted." They weren't busy at the time, so Bill offered, and he and Lester painted the house for him. Lester told Ken Morrison this story years later. When Ken asked him why they would take time out from the more profitable work of importing liquor to go and paint someone's house, Lester replied, "We did it because we weren't busy days at the time, and besides he was sort of our boss."

Joe Tocco's main residence, which was located in one of Wyandotte's more exclusive neighborhoods, would be almost totally destroyed by a series of explosions on February 25, 1932. When fire marshals evaluated the blast, they opined the cause was arson, and a bomb was suspected early on. According to newspaper accounts, their suspicions were further aroused when they discovered that all the really expensive furnishings had been removed prior to the series of explosions that were heard by neighbors. The cheap stuff was left in the house to burn up.

Chapter 6

Finding a Place to Roost

BILL PIPER NARROWLY SURVIVED the gunshot wound. As he slowly mended, he feared for his personal survival, especially if he stayed around Wyandotte, and he was worried that another attempt would be made on his life. Bill was also seriously concerned about the safety of his wife. As soon as he had recovered enough to travel, he and Frances slipped out of Wyandotte, pulling their small house trailer with a canoe secured on top of it. The couple always enjoyed their leisure time traveling in this rig and they once had taken it as far as Colorado on vacation. This time things were much different. Bill Piper was on the lam. He knew full well the violent capabilities of his assailants. If they wanted him out of the way they had a long reach, and would discover him wherever he fled. Lester Piper would lay low and remain in Wyandotte to protect their property and wind down the bootlegging operation and their other business interests. Bill had had it and he was out of the liquor importation business. He and Frances were headed south to find a place to hide until the heat was off. He was at a crossroads and had to come up with a plan to begin a new life.

Bill Piper was an avid fisherman most all of his life. Next to chasing women, as a young man, fishing was his favorite sport. He had fished many of the hot spots in Florida and recalled a remote, yet familiar place where he knew he could hide and literally disappear . . . a place where he and Frances could lay low for a few months and he would have time to figure out what his next move would be.

The hideout was located at an out-of-the-way place known as Dead Lakes. This is a unique area that is located in the Florida Panhandle, about eighty miles south of the Alabama border to the southwest of Tallahassee. It's some twenty-one miles, as the crow flies, north of the popular tourist-filled beaches of the Gulf of Mexico. The Dead Lakes themselves are situated just north of the town of Wewahitchka, in Gulf County, Florida. The Pipers set-up their camp in this secluded spot; it was tucked just far enough away from mainstream traffic and the town that Bill felt safe.

Bill and Frances relaxed while he slowly healed. On the days Bill felt good and when he was in the mood he would spend hours fishing on the nearby Dead Lakes. After Bill had fully recuperated, they left their hideout haven and began to mosey south down the Florida peninsula. On a whim, Bill decided to stop and visit a man that he had met and become acquainted with during one of his earlier trips to Florida. They would stop in Silver Springs, near Ocala, and spend some time with Ross Allen.

Ensill Ross Allen was born in Pittsburg, Pennsylvania, in 1908. Ross, who never used his Christian name, had a great interest in reptiles and crocodilians since his childhood and he had turned into quite a showman. It was only natural he would end up in Florida and connected to the popular Silver Springs attraction near Ocala. He had opened Ross Allen's Reptile Institute, at Silver Springs, in 1929. The Institute quickly became one of the core attractions at the popular springs, which as a whole attracted many visitors. After Bill Piper saw that since his last visit Ross' operation had turned into a financial success, he wanted to become involved. Despite the downturn in the economy as the Great Depression impacted the nation, carloads of tourists continued to seek the winter warmth of Florida and were coming into the state in droves. After Bill offered his assistance to Ross Allen the Pipers decided to remain in Silver Springs for a time and Bill started helping Ross in the day-to-day operation of the Institute. He learned such skills as proper reptilian care, handling and milking venomous snakes like huge and potentially deadly eastern diamondback rattlesnakes, and capturing and handling immense American alligators.

Ross Allen milking a large eastern diamondback rattlesnake at his Reptile Institute.

It was here, under the mentorship of Ross Allen, that Bill Piper rekindled his own childhood interest in wild creatures. Bill totally admired and supported Ross Allen's operation and he soaked in all the experience he was able to acquire because of their close relationship. Bill liked the area around Ocala, so he and Frances, with Ross and his wife Virginia as their partners, bought forty acres of land to the east of Silver Springs in June of 1936. Bill kept a ledger[15]. In it he recorded that, in 1935, he and Ross each made personal investments to develop a "reptile farm[16]" that would specialize in the sale of live reptiles — a new business, separate and independent from Ross' Reptile Institute — that Bill would manage. That journal shows that they each invested $1,626.53 between April, 1935 and November, 1936. They hired local labor and built a house, fenced the property, and had a water well installed. Soon their animal farm was up and running and they began purchasing live specimens from a network of regional collectors. In just two days, on August 25 and 27, 1936, they purchased 1,191 baby alligators and bought hundreds[17] more before the final entry was made in this ledger on December 25, 1936, when it is noted that they purchased their last lot of baby alligators; fifty in all. It appeared that Bill was fully intending to stay put and settle near Silver Springs, but all of a sudden, and because of some now unknown reason, he changed his mind and severed his business relationship with Ross Allen. I suggest that they split because the business simply wasn't turning a profit. It was all investment and little actual income. According to an article that appeared in Volume 33 of the Koreshan Unity's[18] weekly newspaper, "The American Eagle", as late as 1937 they still had forty-seven alligators on the property, but the investment had not paid Bill any dividends. Bill and Frances Piper decided not to stay in the area after all and they moved on south. Bill and Frances sold their interest in the Marion County property in late 1939. Ross and Virginia Allen divorced in 1949.

As a teenager, Bill had lived in Miami with his parents and siblings during their earlier time in Florida. When he and Frances decided the time was right to leave Silver Springs, he said his temporary good-byes to Ross Allen, and the Pipers slowly drifted down the east coast to spend a few weeks in the vicinity of Miami. While living in Dade County, Bill and Frances became reacquainted with old friends and befriended many residents. He looked up and reconnected to the Whittle family who were now living in Coral Gables. Bill knew this family because their paths had once crossed while they were all living in the Saint Petersburg area. Bill would continue to keep in touch with the Whittles, and he made it a point to visit them whenever he was in the vicinity of Miami on business. As the years slipped by, these visits would become more frequent, and in the future this friendship would eventually result in another major change in Bill Piper's life.

The section of the two-lane Tamiami Trail that connected Miami and Naples had opened in 1928. It bisected the Florida Everglades and tied the Miami area to the Florida west coast. Its popular name was derived from the fact that the highway connected the major cities Tampa and Miami. On earlier Florida fishing trips Bill had discovered that the borrow canal along the roadway, and other drainage canals that connected to it, were great fishing spots and also home to a variety of interesting South Florida snakes. During high seasonal water levels, Bill found the Everglades, both south and north of the Trail, to be accessible by canoe. He explored the vast saw grass, the tree islands, and tropical hardwood hammocks of the southern Everglades. He was fascinated by this unique ecosystem and spent many happy days fishing and catching enormous largemouth bass and a variety of snakes. Memories of deadly Wyandotte and the Detroit River where beginning to wane. But, Bill Piper was still restless and eventually the need to move on to new vistas eventually returned, took hold, and his wanderlust drew him back to the open road. Bill and Frances Piper struck out west across the Tamiami Trail.

The expanse of the Everglades passage was spectacular as Bill navigated his panel truck and the connected trailer rig on the straight trail immediately to the east of Miami. It was a straight shot and the alignment of the highway didn't vary until they reached the right-hand curve of Forty-Mile Bend. They stopped and took a break at Monroe Station, one of the way stations along the Tamiami Trail. These fuel and rest stops were spaced about twenty miles apart, and had assigned motorcycle patrolmen to serve disabled motorists traveling the Trail. The couple enjoyed the change in scenery. By the time they reached Monroe Station, they had entered the eastern periphery of the Big Cypress Swamp and the terrain was changing. The Pipers were seeing this part of wild Florida almost ten years before logging interests launched their invasion that would lead to the near devastation of the virgin cypress timber. Their earlier panorama of small tree islands and saw grass of the eastern Everglades had been replaced with huge stands of tall cypress trees. Two decades later, Bill Piper would be involved in a nation-wide battle to save some of the remaining Big Cypress.

They stopped and took another break to look at the beautiful Turner River, where Bill had fished in 1931, before they moved on west again. By the time they reached Carnestown, to the north of Everglades City, the roadway became more undulating, twisting and turning as it meandered through the continuous wetlands. They passed through huge expanses of treeless prairies and southward-reaching fingers of untouched primeval cypress forests. Notably among them was the Fakahatchee Strand, where the ivory-billed woodpecker still lived.

Near the coast and about sixteen miles north of Naples they drove into a quaint but familiar hamlet, the City of Bonita Springs[19]. The ambiance of this small town always seemed idyllic to the Pipers. Bill and Lester had fallen in love with the place a few years earlier. Bill arranged to rent a trailer space at the friendly and popular Baird's Camp and they set up housekeeping. This primitive campground was located on the south side of the Imperial River with frontage on the Tamiami Trail. After a few days, having settled in, the Pipers decided to extend their stay in the community indefinitely.

The headwaters of the beautiful Imperial River were about four miles to the east in the wetlands of the Big Cypress. After the river flowed past Baird's Camp and ducked under the highway bridge, it meandered unobstructed about seven miles through the pine woods and red mangroves until it reached the shallow estuary of southern Estero Bay. Water flowing down the Imperial River ultimately reached the Gulf of Mexico through two passes; Big Hickory Pass to the north and Little Hickory Pass to the south. Bill Piper had fished these passes in the past and found them to be exceptionally productive for tough game fish like snook.

Bill began to scout the inland countryside hoping to locate the best places to fish and he was pleased he had his choice of either fresh or salt-water species. He also spent hours canoeing the Imperial River and its creek tributaries to observe snakes, alligators, and turtles. He listened intently as townspeople told him where he could find, or see, this or that animal or bird. He befriended many local residents. Among them were two

Photo courtesy of Anna Piper Mackereth.

Bill and Frances Piper during happy laid-back days in Bonita Springs, in 1934. Bill holds Florida softshell turtles and Francis holds snapping turtles caught in his turtle traps.

experienced woodsmen, Stanley Whidden and Luther McCormick. These men became his field companions and in their company Bill made treks out into the Big Cypress Swamp on foot or in a cut-down Model-A Ford with oversized tires. He let it be known around town, and in his letters back home to his family in Michigan, that he planned to extend his stay in Florida and later hoped to relocate to Bonita Springs. Frances was not too happy when Bill started talking about putting down roots.

Shortly after hearing about Bill's failed reptile farm near Silver Springs, Lester suggested that the two of them should pool together and start their own reptile exhibit somewhere in Florida. Bill couldn't help but notice the steady stream of traffic that flowed through the town in both directions as touring motorists traveled up and down the Tamiami Trail. Despite the reality that the Great Depression was at its worst, those that had the spending money still vacationed in Florida. The Tamiami Trail was the only arterial access for folks that were traveling down the Gulf coast headed for the well-advertised Southeast Florida tourism destinations in and around Miami. Baird's Camp and other tourist-dependant businesses on the busy highway were doing very well. Bill Piper got a brainstorm — or should I call it a revelation — that he continued to mull around in his head . . . working out the rough details before he would share his idea with Frances. When he was ready, he told her that he thought that Bonita Springs would be a perfect place to establish a tourist attraction like Lester had suggested. He was thinking of something modeled after Ross Allen's Reptile Institute at Silver Springs. He told Frances that the people traveling the Trail were hungry for information and looking for places to spend their money. A tourist attraction would be just the place to entertain and educate them and help relieve them of some of their vacation cash. He began researching the steps that he would have to take to accomplish such a feat.

When Bill and Frances snuck back into Wyandotte, Prohibition was just about finished. It would be repealed upon the full ratification of the Twenty-first Amendment on December 5, 1933. Bill and Lester's low-key life of crime was coming to an end. The killing spree in the Wyandotte area was over and the heat was off because gang rivalries were winding down. Those bootleggers, like the Piper brothers who had saved piles of money, began to move into the legitimate business sector. Bill and Lester talked constantly about the concept of a Florida wildlife-oriented tourist attraction. The brothers returned to Bonita Springs together with their wives the next year, in 1933, and that trip convinced them this is where they were meant to be. They decided to consolidate their capital and proceed with developing and opening their exhibit that featured the wildlife of the Everglades in Bonita Springs. They agreed to form a partnership entirely based on their mutual verbal agreement, with nothing put down in writing on paper. Lester's interest in wild animals had never slackened since their childhood, and when they made this commitment, neither of them stopped to consider the load of responsibility they would ultimately be heaping on their shoulders.

Chapter 7

In the Beginning

IN 1934 THERE WERE no reptile or wildlife oriented tourist attractions in Southwest Florida. The very successful Saint Augustine Alligator Farm had opened in 1893, Ross Allen's Reptile Institute at Silver Springs, in 1929, the McKee Jungle Gardens at Vero Beach in 1932, and the Sarasota Reptile Farm and Zoo had opened its doors in the mid-thirties. Bill and Lester Piper had decided to launch a business venture and make a commitment. They would open an attraction in Bonita Springs and exhibit wildlife that occurred in the Everglades. And, they would enjoy collecting most of the specimens themselves. After all, they considered themselves to be retired and this would give them something to do with their time.

Bill and Frances Piper, again pulling their trailer, returned to Bonita Springs in late 1936 to finalize the deal on the purchase of some property on which he and his brother Lester had negotiated a sales contract. Lester traveled to Bonita Springs by bus, and after arrangements were made for the initial real estate transaction, he returned to Wyandotte to wind down his personal business interests and find renters for his and Bill's real estate holdings there. He was also awaiting the birth of his first and only child. Lester and Lucille's son, David Thomas Piper, was born in Wyandotte, Michigan, on August 11, 1935.

The brothers had negotiated the purchase of Lots 1 to 6, inclusive, of Block C of the Spring Gardens Subdivision in downtown Bonita Springs. The transaction closed on May 25, 1937. This parcel had highway frontage, plus its southern boundary was the Imperial River. They also secured an option to purchase Block B of Spring Gardens Subdivision. They had made their first step and would complete the purchase of Block B in 1940. The grouped-lot parcel they eventually owned contained eleven lots and fronted on the Tamiami Trail. A deeded street, Johnson Avenue, separated the two parcels that were platted as Blocks B and C of Bonita Farms, a subdivision originally filed with the Clerk of the Circuit Court, Lee County, in 1912. The 1925 plat of Spring Gardens shows that the rear, or western edge of the parcels, was bounded by the right of way of the Fort Myers Southern Railroad. A few years later, in 1943, Bill and Lester would also purchase Lots 7 through 12 of the Riverside subdivision. These parcels were across the 130-foot wide railroad right of way, to the west of Block B and C of Spring Gardens Subdivision, on Riverside Drive. These lots were most likely originally purchased by the Pipers to provide an additional buffer for the Gardens and to later make the eventual vacating of Johnson Avenue in the Piper's favor more palatable for the Lee County Commission. Bill and Frances would stay in Bonita Springs and he started the grueling work to clear the property.

The first City of Bonita Springs had become a financial nightmare and its ruling city council voted to dissolve the city and requested that the Florida Legislature rescind their City Charter. The Legislature concurred and Bonita Springs again became a part of unincorporated Lee County, in 1935. This was an opportune time for the Pipers to launch development of their tourist attraction because they would have to deal with the regulations of just one layer of local government.

When grouped together, the two blocks and the right of way of Johnson Street that would later be vacated by Lee County, totaled 3.72 acres. The terrain of the combined parcels was generally low and could best be described as pine flatwoods. The elevation of the land was about the same as the highway, and along its southern boundary it dropped off about ten feet as it sloped down to the Imperial River. Large slash pines, cabbage palms, and palmettos were the primary vegetative types on the property, with a mix of small live oaks and leather ferns as the elevation descended along the bank of the river. When Lester arrived in Bonita Springs, the first order of business was for the brothers to finish the labor intensive and slow process of clearing their property. They did this by hand with the use of machetes, axes, and hand-powered saws. When this was done, they hired Luther McCormick who had a dump truck to begin hauling in fill and boulders to raise the ground elevation along the riverfront. They soon decided this method was taking much too long so they eliminated truck-hauling the fill and hired Norman Slater who owned a small hydraulic dredge. He moved his rig upriver and pumped spoil from the river bottom to raise the grade of the property while Luther McCormick continued to haul riprap to form a steeply angled stone retaining wall. This would armor the new fill along the edge of the river to resist erosion.

While the grading of the property continued, Bill and Lester hired some local carpenters to help them and started work on a large frame entrance building. The lumber that was used for construction of this building and most of the original cages came from an abandoned house that they bought for $25.00, in 1938. The building was located on a nice lot along the Imperial River, and years later, in a mood of hindsight, Bill complained because they hadn't bought the land, too. The Pipers and their hired carpenters demolished the house and recycled the lumber. This new building would serve as a gift shop and museum, and also provide living space for Lester and Lucille. Since arriving in Bonita Springs they had been renting a small cabin across the river at the Imperial River Court and would live there during, and for a time after the completion of their apartment. Bill and Frances continued to live in their small house trailer.

There was no written master plan for future development of the property. The Bonita Springs Reptile Gardens would remain a work in progress to be modified as needed and as space allowed. Exhibits, pens, and cages would be fabricated as required to cope with the growth of the collection. As a Bonita Springs resident recalled during an interview in 2009, "The Bonita Springs Reptile Gardens was just a hole in the ground at first."

Just as soon as the property was uniformly brought up to grade and leveled, work started on a fence that would extend around the perimeter of the grounds, or the yard, as it would be called later. This was an important addition for a variety of reasons. A fence would keep people from wandering into the compound and prevent most aquatic and terrestrial forms of wildlife from leaving the property should they ever manage to escape their cage or enclosure. When the grounds within the fence was later landscaped, it would rustically mesh into the design and display a lush tropical ambiance.

Bill and Lester decided that their fence would be a simple and attractive stockade made from cypress poles. The supporting posts were stout lighter heart pine. They were extremely hard and insect-proof uprights. The fence posts and stockade poles were readily available and basically free for the taking in and around the many cypress heads near Bonita Springs. The posts were purchased from outside suppliers and were relatively inexpensive. A few families in Bonita Springs scraped out a meager living cutting the heart pine fence posts out in the Big Cypress Swamp. Over the next couple of years thousands of cypress saplings were harvested by the Pipers and brought to the Gardens. They were boiled and debarked before being added to the fence.

Soon after the building was finished, the Imperial River flooded. Water from the rain-swollen waterway rose to within inches of flooding the floor of the structure. The wise decision was made to raise the building because of the threat that future flood events posed. Lester wiggled through the low crawl space to position heavy railroad jacks, and the structure was slowly and methodically lifted to the new elevation. Additional weight-bearing concrete piers were inserted to support the building at its new elevation, and when all were in place, the structure was lowered to rest on them. The Imperial River has overflowed its banks several times since the entrance building was raised, but never at a high enough flood stage to put standing water above the floor level.

They needed a reliable water source to supply the voluminous amounts of water that would be necessary to fill the many pens they eventually hoped to have in place. Water was also needed for landscape irrigation and general utilitarian uses in the buildings and living quarters. A total of five artesian wells were drilled on the property to provide the necessary amount of water. These were very deep wells, often hundreds of feet in depth, that reached an underground stratum of pressurized water, that when tapped, produced a remarkable head pressure up at the ground surface. This natural artesian pressure aided in getting the flowing water distributed where needed.

An early postcard from the author's collection.

A Doubleday postcard, from 1938, shows the entrance building just after construction and before it was elevated, and the attraction's first sign. The Model-A to the right is Lester Piper's. The slash pines in the background would soon be replaced by a variety of exotic tropical fruit trees and plants.

This well water also had the advantage that it had a constant year-round temperature of about seventy-two degrees[20], which would benefit some animals during the winter. Certainly the American crocodiles, which are not very cold tolerant, would be direct beneficiaries. The downside of this artesian water was its odor. It smelled terrible because of the sulphurous dioxide gas associated with the liquid once it reached the surface and the gas billowed into the atmosphere. When first entering the Gardens and stepping up to a crocodilian pen, many customers who had never been exposed to the rotten egg odor of artesian sulfur water, found it downright disgusting. Those who could not cope with the bad odor even gagged. Residents of Bonita Springs took the odor in stride since the same quality of water was used in their households.

There was no community water system in play at the time that distributed treated potable water in the city. After long exposure to sulfur water people adjusted and it became basically unnoticeable. However, some people had the misconception when first entering the Gardens that the odor must have been related to dirty cages and general unclean conditions. The smell was that bad.

In 1937, Ross Allen talked Bill into going along with him on a collecting trip to Central America. Bill thought it would be an adventure, so he agreed to make the trip with his friend. They booked passage aboard an empty freighter that was leaving Tampa for a return voyage to British Honduras[21] for another load of bananas. Once in Central America they would hunt crocodiles along the coast and then fly to Honduras for a few days to get into the wild mountainous country of the interior where they hoped to collect snakes and other reptiles. On arriving in British Honduras, they discovered they would have a one-week delay before their scheduled airplane flight[22] would leave for Honduras. To be ready to go into the field, they took advantage of this delay and received precautionary inoculations against cholera, diphtheria, and typhoid. Otherwise, they filled their days by going afield in search of local amphibians and reptiles. For the most part, collecting was poor, but finally they got a lead from a local resident as to where they could go to possibly catch crocodiles. This turned into an adventure after the pair found the difficult to reach place and, borrowing a dugout canoe, launched it after dark into a lagoon where they observed the reflecting eyes of a few crocodiles. The larger crocodiles were timid, but the smaller ones would freeze when the beam of Bill and Ross' battery-powered headlamps was directed into their eyes. After the men had slowly paddled very close to one of the young crocodiles, trying not to spook it, Ross reached out to grab the four-foot specimen. As he leaned, overextending his reach, his weight shift threw the craft off balance. The dugout capsized and both men went overboard into the tepid, dark, muddy water. Ross came back to the surface first. He looked around and didn't see Bill anywhere in sight; just his Stetson hat floating on the surface. Suddenly, sputtering and splashing, Bill Piper rose above the surface of the lagoon. They managed to get the canoe ashore, bailed it out, and returned to the crocodile hunt. Before the night was over, and after several trips to the land and back to unload bags of crocodiles, they managed to bag a total of twenty-two specimens.

Finally, they flew to Honduras and hiked into the mountains along with a donkey train. After several days they encountered their first venomous snake. Ross Allen described this event in a 1950 interview[23]. "It was a fer-de-lance which resembles a diamondback (rattlesnake) both in general appearance and disposition. It was on a hillside, and Bill Piper's first sight of it gave him quite a start. The fer-de-lance was going someplace, in no special haste, just at a leisurely pace. But when Bill rushed past, hurrying along, the startled snake shot out its wicked head in a strike that missed Bill by mere inches. The snake was on the higher side of the slope, and the force of its blow brought its body directly across my path."

Ross pinned and caught the fer-de-lance and they continued on their way. Over the next few days they also collected more of this species, as well as a few boa constrictors, a variety of smaller snakes, a few iguanas, several dozen large cane toads, twenty basilisk lizards, and a variety of fresh water turtles. They culled the crocodiles down to ten specimens and traveled back to British Honduras with these and everything else they had collected. The pair of weary travelers returned to Florida on another banana boat.

In Bill Piper's view the Central American trip was a flop, and according to him, Ross Allen ended up with all of the specimens they jointly collected. In 1986, while being videotaped, Bill commented, "He didn't have too much fun and I didn't either. Yeah, we had some snakes. Ross ended up with everything and he took them up there to Silver Springs. We went this way and that way, and first thing I knew he got them all. Ross was kind of that way. One time I said, 'Ross you're kind of tight.' One of the guys who worked for him said, 'Tight?, Bill? He'd skin his grandmother if he could sell the hide!' He was straightening nails and I asked him what the hell he was doing? He said, 'Ross told me to straighten them.' And that's exactly what he was doing with a pail of rusty nails." The argument over the distribution of their specimens from their herpetological collecting expedition to Central America may have been the final disagreement that disconnected the close friendship of the two men.

Lester Piper found out early on that he had a green thumb, and soon he became an outstanding horticulturist. He obtained and introduced a variety of exotic fruiting and flowering trees and shrubs to the yard of the Gardens. He had learned the art of grafting and produced a colorful variety of crotons and hibiscus that were used to line the walkways to help steer patrons along the route to connect with guided tours that were in progress. Heart pine railings along the walkways kept people on the concrete and protected the shrubbery from foot traffic and concrete walkways directed pedestrian flow. After landscaping, the walkway gave the impression to customers they were experiencing a much larger facility than what they were actually walking through.

David Piper recalled an episode when a Gardens employee observed a visitor who was in the process of cutting some of Lester's prized flowers. He ran and found Lester and told him what he had seen. Lester ran out in the yard and caught the man in the act. There were some harsh words spoken and in the end Lester physically removed the culprit from the Gardens with the added admonishment, "Don't you ever come back in here!"

One room in the gift shop/entrance building was used as a small museum and it housed a collection of natural history specimens and Native American artifacts[24]. During their early years in Bonita Springs the Piper brothers explored the ancient Calusa Indian sites that were scattered along the coast. Like everyone else during that period, they dug in the mounds to search for artifacts. They displayed their best finds in display cases in their small museum, along with mammalian and crocodilian skulls and formalin-filled jars holding preserved amphibians, snakes, lizards, turtles, crocodilians, and fish. A few mounted birds and mammals were also part of the museum. The gift shop offered Seminole and Miccosukee Indian crafts, including beautifully sewn jackets, dolls, and other Indian craft items for sale. Turtle shells, and mounted crocodilian hides and snakeskins were displayed along the upper walls of the gift shop, but these were not offered for sale. The Bonita Springs Reptile Gardens obtained the first of its Lee County Occupational Licenses (2) on November 3, 1938.

Photo courtesy of Anna Piper Mackereth.

From the left; Lester, Lucille, Frances, and Bill. This image is from a 1938 Christmas card issued to family and friends by Bonita Springs Reptile Gardens.

The loud arguments sometimes overheard between Bill and Lester was legendary. Alfred Trew was present early one morning when Lester found out that Bill had gone out snake hunting all night instead of showing up on time to help mix and pour concrete for the bases of a long row of new cages for bears and panthers they had under construction along the back of the yard. Lester was furious because Bill hadn't shown up on time to do his share of the work. When Bill finally arrived on the job several hours late, Lester lit into him with such a tirade that the confrontation quickly came to blows and the two brothers squared off in a short-lived fistfight. Everyone in the work crew just stood and watched. No one dared to step in and try to stop the fray. The brothers traded blows and wrestled around until they each had enough and was winded. Over and done with, and the anger out of their systems, they went to work.

By the early forties, as her life in Bonita Springs dragged on, Frances Piper was becoming increasingly unhappy. She and Bill had been married for more than fifteen years and Francis had been unable to conceive a child. She knew that Bill had always hoped for children. Her husband was now more preoccupied with his work than ever, as he laboriously struggled to build his dream. She perceived this to mean that his work was more important to him than she was. They were spending less and less time together nurturing their marriage and it was literally falling apart around them. Everyone knew this, and to Alfred Trew it was obvious what was happening to one of his favorite people — the woman who had kindly nursed him through his snakebites. Frances became increasingly more distressed when her husband began to tighten their purse strings and she was forced to forgo things that she wanted. Her needs were not extravagant, just womanly material goods that they could easily have afforded. Frances knew full well that there was no reason for Bill to become a total penny pincher, but judging by his behavior he was moving in that direction. By 1942, Frances also suspected that her husband was having an extramarital affair. Trying to escape the lifestyle, she occasionally ran away from Bonita Springs, trying to break away and leave Bill. Whenever they argued and she felt hopeless, she would leave her husband. But without any support, Frances Piper was forced to return to what she perceived as her boring, isolated life with Bill in Bonita Springs.

Things soon worsened for Frances after she and her brother-in-law, Lester, argued over a silly aspect of business operations at the Bonita Springs Reptile Gardens. She and Lester's wife, Lucille, shared duties. They worked in the gift store and sold tickets at the entrance to the steady stream of visitors who paid the 28-cent fee for entry into the Gardens. The entrance fee was a quarter, but then there was a required three-cent tax tacked onto that. Frances was good with numbers and had a background in accounting, so she did the books for the Bonita Springs Reptile Gardens — the Piper brothers' partnership. One evening Lester decided he wanted to take a look at the books, claiming he had been somewhat remiss in reviewing their income and expenditures. As he slowly turned the pages and scanned Frances' neat handwritten columns, his repressed criminal mindset must have kicked in. Lester suddenly stopped staring at the ledger, looked up at Bill and then turned his head to look at Frances, asking, "What the hell are we paying out so much money in taxes for? Can't we fudge on the amount we report . . . just a little bit?"

Frances, trying to be professional, was flabbergasted at his remark, and answered, "Bill . . . You can't do that, Lester! If you two suddenly don't pay enough in taxes, that'll send the revenue office a signal and they'll come here and do an audit and catch up with you. You'll lose your licenses and they'll make you shut this place down." Bill was silent on the issue. It was Lester who spoke up again and told her he didn't want to hear that crap from her. He was sure no one would discover if they raked a few pennies off the top now and then. Frances Piper refused to be part of such a conspiracy and let Lester know that in no uncertain terms. Lester got the last word in and made a few wisecracks that disgruntled Frances further. She now was dead sure she wanted out of her situation, but how?

Alfred Trew had moved to Bonita Springs from New York State with his parents and siblings in early 1936. He was sixteen years of age when he arrived in town and soon was among a group of local teenagers who regularly hung around to watch the progress of the soon to be opened Bonita Springs Reptile Gardens. Bill Piper took a liking to the boy. After he learned the Trew family was having a difficult time making ends meet, he gave Alfred a place to sleep and saw to it that he was fed. Over seventy years later, Alfred remembered, "It was almost like Bill had adopted me." This was at the height of the Depression and nearly everyone in Bonita Springs was financially stretched thin. The Pipers got their fair share out of their investment in Alfred Trew. The teenager still attended school and was a very good student. Unlike his mentor he would stick with his education and graduate from high school — in Fort Myers.

Bill and Lester decided that their new enterprise should feature personalized guided tours. This way the behavior of customers in the yard could be monitored and they would receive an accurate interpretation of the Gardens and the wildlife of the Everglades, and detailed information about the wildlife species they were seeing, up close and personal. When Bonita Springs Reptile Gardens officially opened for business[25], Alfred Trew became the first in a long line of guides who would represent the Piper brothers for over a half-century. The Gardens opened during the days of racial segregation in the south and all of the guides over the years would be Caucasian. That is with one exception, the Pipers hired a black man from Fort Myers as their guide in the 1940s. His name was Robert Burns. He was a popular Gardens personality and did a very good job.

Alfred was already getting his room and board so he guided for tips. He did a good job. The customers appreciated his messages, and tipped him reasonably well. During his high school years, the tips bought his clothes, school supplies, and put some change in his pocket. As long as people were coming into the Gardens, the tours were continuous. After paying the fee and entering, visitors would be directed by Lucille or Frances to where the guide was located at that moment, and instructed to join in with his group. When they had made the complete loop of exhibits and reached the point where they had first joined the tour, their walk-through was over.

The first salaried guide at the Gardens was Charles Normandie, a Bonita Springs winter resident. According to Bill Piper's ledger he paid "Charlie" $8.75 per week in 1940.

Chapter 8

Not So Dear, Deer

MOST OF THE WHITE-TAILED deer population in South Florida in 1935 was infected with fever ticks that transmitted a protozoan pathogen. The ticks were vectors of bovine piroplasmosis. When the tiny arachnids attached themselves to domestic livestock they transmitted this disease, which quickly debilitated cattle by destroying the host animal's red blood cells. Infected cows developed extremely high fevers and most soon died. Over time, Florida scrub cattle had managed to develop a level of immunity to this disease. However, cattlemen who were trying to improve the lot of their livestock could not introduce new breeds into their herds with hopes of improving beef production and quality. This tick fever impacted the burgeoning Florida livestock industry, and a move was made by the Florida Legislature to eradicate the responsible tick species in the state.

Researchers had found if cattle were dipped into an arsenic solution the ticks would die and dislodge before they could mature, drop off, and lay eggs on the ground. Properly spaced periodic dipping would interfere with the responsible tick's life cycle and over time the frequent dipping should eliminate the problem. In 1923, the Florida Legislature enacted a mandatory dipping program, and dipping vats were constructed in areas throughout the state. The program was started in North Florida in 1923, and each year the program expanded southward and eventually reached Southwest Florida in the 1930s. Barbed wire fencing was erected to isolate each dipping area and its vat, when a dipping vat site was added to the network and became a part of the southward expanding program. The Thad Williams family, who owned a large ranching operation between Bonita Springs and Estero, drove their herd of cattle to the dipping facility that was located near today's West Terry Street, on the north side of Bonita Springs. The Williams herd was dipped on the schedule mandated by the state regulators.

Since deer could not be rounded up and dipped Florida launched a deer-killing program that was aimed at removing deer from the equation. An absence of deer would help prevent the spread of cattle-tick fever. Between 1939 and 1941, the Florida Fish and Wildlife Conservation Commission estimates that contract hunters in South Florida destroyed a minimum of ten thousand deer. By 1944, south Florida was finally declared tick fever free and the Florida Legislature approved funding of $25,000.00 per year to introduce tick-fever free deer into the state. Many were purchased from a Wisconsin game farm and transported to southern Florida for restocking. White-tailed deer eventually made a comeback throughout Florida.

Many orphaned fawns were brought to the Pipers during the years that deer were being slaughtered by the large-scale hunting program. The remaining Piper herd may be nearly genetically pure original Florida white-tailed stock because of their origins from those orphaned fawns that ended up at the early Gardens and were successfully treated for tick infestations in the 1930s. The small deer were hand-raised, and eventually a large deeryard was fenced off for the growing herd of whitetails. Before long, the deer were reproducing and the captive herd became self-sustaining.

Several fawns were produced each year and the confined herd slowly increased beyond what Lester considered capacity. To balance the captive population and make it more manageable, once fawns matured they were periodically scheduled for release. Many were used to reintroduce white-tailed deer into areas where the natural population was considered thin. For example, in late 1955, the Piper brothers turned over seven buck deer to Walter Whitehead. He lived in Fort Myers and was the area supervisor for the Florida Game and Freshwater Fish Commission. These captive-raised deer were turned loose in the Six-Mile Cypress, near Fort Myers.

The Everglades Wonder Gardens deer herd at feeding time, 1956. The buck is in velvet. Wild turkeys and a sandhill crane (to right with head down) share the yard.

Most people, when around deer, consider the animals to be much like the Bambi characterization produced and made famous by Walt Disney. Others consider them to be docile per the persona of "Flag" in *The Yearling*. The Piper brothers soon learned from experience what we know today — that white-tailed deer are among the most dangerous wild animals inhabiting North America. As a whole, they are potentially far more dangerous to people than bears, alligators, or rattlesnakes. Aggressive white-tailed deer in America seriously injure dozens of people each year, and sometimes these interactions result in human mortality.

Male white-tailed deer rub away and completely remove the velvet-like living tissue, which temporarily covers their growing antlers during their annual repetitive development. When the antler bone matures, even the tamest of buck deer change their personality when entering their rutting season — become sexually aroused — and feel their hormone-loaded power. The dominant buck among the captive Gardens herd occasionally would stalk and attack staff members who were assigned to their daily care and feeding. It was extremely dangerous at times to enter the deeryard to rake and clean it, make repairs or improvements, or provide food and water. Not only were the antlers of the deer dangerous, but a really excited buck would use a combination of antlers and hooves to inflict damage on whatever he perceived to be an adversary — fellow deer or caregiver. Open wounds could be the result should two bucks become engaged in a duel. Blood would usually attract egg-laden screwworm flies, so for the safety of the workers and the health of the herd antler amputation was in order.

The biggest and strongest person on staff was called on to launch the procedure that would usually be scheduled near the end of the day, after the guide had passed the deeryard on his last tour of the day. This operation was best done out of public view. Four or five people had to be involved to pull the procedure off safely. In the early days Lester Piper usually took the lead position. In later years Don Carroll, or Lester's son, David, both big men, would take up the challenge. The initial assignment for the lead person was to antagonize and get the target buck to launch an attack. As the animal charged, the person being assaulted had to be ready to reach out and grab hold of both antlers. He would then then force the deer's head down to prevent it from kicking forward high enough to slash the catcher with its front hooves. The remainder of the group would then dive in, grab deer body parts, and carefully wrestle the buck to the ground. With the deer now held firmly against the ground, but still trying to free itself, a hacksaw would be presented with which the antlers would be removed, one by one. Then a coarse file would be used to round over and smooth the edges of the boney stubs. The subdued deer was then released to rejoin his on-looking harem. Although now less majestic in appearance, the buck was undaunted as he resumed his role as chief stud.

There was always some confusion when Gardens patrons first viewed the small deer herd. Bear in mind that the majority of visitors were northerners who were touring the Florida vacationland. Most were familiar with the more robust, much larger northern race of white-tailed deer. An average northern white-tailed buck will tip the scales at two hundred three pounds; an average-sized Florida white-tailed buck reaches one hundred twenty-five pounds. So, immediately, many thought those at the Gardens were the even smaller Florida key deer, which have an average weight of only eighty pounds. Guides soon learned that as part of their spiel they had to be sure to explain that the small deer in the Gardens collection were not the rare and range-restricted "toy" deer of the Florida Keys.

Chapter 9

Stars of the Show

MANY OF THE WILD animals that were housed in the collection at the Gardens were special. Some had an individualized unique history and there was usually a good story behind how each of them got there. The Piper brothers' philosophy was best described in their own statement that appeared in a long line of their attraction's brochures.

> "We present the Everglades Reptile Gardens without any particular training in showmanship or exploitation. Years of actual experience and contact with wildlife have given us an intimate knowledge of their habits that we wish to share with you. We have only a sincere desire to give the visitor a clear picture of the thrilling life, dangers, intrigue and constant struggle for existence that goes on in the depths of the impenetrable and fascinating Everglades.
>
> Sincerely,
> Wilford and Lester Piper"

In the early days of the Reptile Gardens, proper care and feeding of the animals, birds, reptiles, and crocodilians in the collection was the main goal. This would remain the most important issue on Lester Piper's plate for the rest of his life. Nothing else in life ever seemed to matter to him, just the animals, although the man did have a few hobbies. He collected commemorative postage stamps and silver dollars. When WINK television began to broadcast in Fort Myers in 1954, Lester absolutely loved to watch the weekly Red Skelton Show.

Constant expansion and improvement of facilities was the theme of every workday and construction of new quarters adequate to house the growing number and variety of specimens was the goal. Bill and Lester and the crew basically worked from dawn until after dark to care for and feed their wildlife wards and keep pace with expansion and maintenance. Acquisition and preparation of food for all the hungry mouths took considerable staff effort and had to be meshed with facilities development so everything clicked. Feeding was a priority and now that the collection was basically complete, new construction would be on the backburner and tackled as time permitted.

In a 1959 interview that was published in the Bonita Banner newspaper, Bill Piper is quoted, "We considered ourselves as retired and figured we could put in a few cages of animals, and charge tourists to see them, while we spent all day hunting and fishing and occasionally bringing in a few new animals. That is the silliest thought I ever had. We have had a 12 hour — seven day a week job ever since."

The Bonita Springs Reptile Gardens hadn't been open long when someone found and brought in an adult bald eagle with an injured wing. The damage to the bone was so extensive that Lester had to amputate the wing extremely close to the bird's body. Bill and Lester cautiously educated themselves and took a practical common-sense approach to wildlife veterinary medicine. For special cases that required more technical or advanced skills than their expertise allowed they relied on a veterinarian in Fort Myers. However, they discovered that few qualified vets knew how to actually treat wild animals. There were very few basic procedures and treatments the Pipers were not qualified to do on their own. In many cases their treatment would be considered crude in today's world, but whatever had to be done was accomplished with caring compassion for the animal being surgically treated, or perhaps rehabilitated following an injury. They always treated their captives humanely, as they utilized proven and successful method-ologies that were based on their personal experience.

Lester and Bill wanted a perfect eagle, one that would be more impressive when it spread its wings, and one that could fly around in the cage. In 1939, after they found that an active bald eagle nest near Bonita Springs contained two eaglets, they swung into action. It was now or never. They knew that federal regulations were being developed to fully protect bald eagles exclusively, and not just because they were migratory birds and already protected by the Migratory Bird Treaty Act between Canada, Mexico, and the United States. This new legislation slowly winding through Congress would become the Bald Eagle Protection Act. It would be implemented on June 8, 1940, and thereafter it would be illegal for anyone to collect or harass the nation's symbol.

Lester and Bill called on their nineteen-year old protégé, Alfred Trew, to do this dangerous and difficult work. He was chosen because he was lighter than they were, more agile for the task at hand, and due to his youth he was always unafraid to tackle tough jobs. From a distance the three examined the enormous stick nest that was positioned high in a slash pine. Bill gave the teenager his instructions. "Strap on these climbing spikes and this belt and climb the tree until you're directly underneath the nest . . . be careful damn it, I don't want you falling and busting your ass. When you get up close to the nest, drop this small line down to us and I'll tie an axe onto it for you to hoist up. Then I want you to chop up through the bottom of the nest and grab one of the young eagles and toss it down to us."

Alfred was totally inexperienced with climbing spurs but he did what he was told and then listened to their shouted instructions as he slowly ascended the big tree shifting the safety belt up the trunk ahead of him as he climbed. They had to speak loudly because the adult eagles were soaring overhead and screaming in discontent about this invasion of their most intimate zone. Bill wanted to make sure that Alfred was jabbing the spurs deep into the tree to support his weight. Although Alfred was also wearing a lineman's safety belt, Bill didn't want a spur to slip. He feared watching the boy fall and skin the bark off the tree and the skin off his body, as he came crashing to the ground trying to hug the tree on his way down. Alfred's confidence built as he climbed higher. He had to reach a point at which the tree forked. The fork supported the nest. With the axe now in his hand, Alfred began to chop through the base of the nest while chips, branches, pieces of dried fish backbones, and dried and dusty eagle excrement rained down on him. He managed to move a little further up the trunk as he hacked through and removed sections of the dead branches that the pair of eagles had used as a foundation to support the heavy nest. Finally, the hole was sufficiently large enough and he reached up and caught one of the prefledgling eagles by one of its legs. He then carefully pulled the bird through the opening he had created through the thick nest. The bird flapped its wings enough to slow its fall as it fell into Bill's waiting arms.

Years later, another bald eagle would become part of the Gardens' collection, but it would never be put in the cage with the other eagles to be placed on public exhibition. Everglades Wonder Gardens had a migratory bird permit issued by the U.S. Fish and Wildlife Service that allowed the Pipers to hold specific species. The number of specimens of each individual species were specified on the permit. They were permitted to have and display only two bald eagles. A rehabilitation permit covered the third eagle, since it had been rescued and was undergoing rehabilitation and was being housed temporarily, preparatory to its release back into the wild population.

Gardens employee Warren Boutchia rescued the third eagle after he discovered the bird completely stuck in a pool of tar that must have been left over from a roofing job and dumped by a dim-witted employee of a roofing company. This was near the shoulder of the Trail just outside of Bonita Springs. A variety of other wildlife species including insects, mice, and other birds had also become inextricably stuck in the soft tar. These species probably attracted the eagle to the site where it thought them easy prey, but instead the bird became hopelessly trapped in the thick tar. Recalling this incident, Warren told me, "This beautiful bird's legs were deep in the tar and its wings and feathers were covered with the black sticky stuff. The feathers were all stuck together. It was a mess. It kept trying to bite me, but I managed to rescue it. I was able to pull it loose from the tar without breaking any of its bones. I held it tight and took it to the Gardens. By the time I got there with it a lot of the tar had transferred to my clothing, and I looked almost as bad as the eagle.

Photo courtesy of Bob Garrison.

Lester Piper releasing the rehabilitated bald eagle in his and Bill's Bonita Spring pasture.

"Lester and I spent several hours washing the tar from its legs, feet, and beak with kerosene. We either cut-off or plucked out its tar-covered feathers. This eagle looked pretty bad when it was placed in a cage outside of the main yard near my sleeping quarters. I gave it special care the whole time it recuperated at the Gardens. Lester turned it loose about a year later and we all had a good feeling inside, knowing this majestic bird survived and we helped it successfully return to the wild."

Now that he was an accredited tree climber, the Pipers soon enlisted Alfred Trew's skill again, after they discovered a fish crow's nest. They wanted a young crow, but they had to wait to snatch it until they were sure the eggs had hatched. When they could see the parents were beginning to feed young birds, they knew it was time to send Alfred aloft. Alfred swung into action and mounted the nest tree. He quickly climbed to the nest, reached in, and took a white down-covered young bird. He put it in a cloth sack, stuck it in his belt, and returned to the ground. This little crow became known as "Jimmy" and over time Jimmy became one of the most popular creatures ever exhibited at the Everglades Wonder Gardens — by whatever of the three names the attraction was known.

Bill concentrated on teaching Jimmy to talk. It's an old wive's tale; you don't have to split a crow's tongue to get it to speak human words and make other sounds. All it takes is almost constant repetition of a person's vocal sounds and the bird will soon be mimicking the human voice to an amazing level of clarity. Crows and starlings are equally skilled in their ability to speak as well as the more touted myna birds or most species of parrots.

One of the first words that Jimmy uttered was, "Alfred!" He picked this up quickly because Lucille and Frances would yell out the guide's name to let him know that people were entering the Gardens for a tour. Before long, Alfred would often hear his name being called and would run to the entrance, anticipating people had just entered and it was time to begin a tour, only to find it was Jimmy calling him. Seventy years later, Alfred Trew told me, "That bird was something else. I'd be out in the yard cleaning cages or something and Jimmy would holler out my name. I'd hear him screaming, 'Alfred!' and thinking it was one of the women I'd start running for the store, expecting to find people waiting."

Bill taught Jimmy a couple of the bird's standard phrases that always thrilled customers. These were, "Now, girls, girls" and "Come open up that bottle, will you!" People would crack up when he turned loose with the latter, but of course sometimes, Jimmy would clam up and just utter standard fish crow sounds. During my time as guide, I learned that if he wouldn't talk after I had coaxed him every which way I could, I'd just move on. After I had explained to my group about Tom the bear, I'd usually tell them, "Now listen carefully," and I'd dash back to Jimmy's cage and quietly begin saying the words. By the time I got to the word "open" Jimmy would bow slightly and turn it loose in full volume, "Come open up that bottle, will you!" That always delighted the people in my group to no end.

"Old man Mose sure is a buster, he ate five dogs and a feather duster!" This piece of prose was penned by Bill Piper in 1956, at a time Lester had us busy refinishing the red and white roadside slat signs that adorned the vista along the Tamiami Trail. Several rhyming lines of copy were added to the sets of signs to tell motorists about the big alligator. Old Man Mose was a good-sized bull alligator, but he wasn't known for his massive size. Mose was kept alone because he was an exceptionally perfect adult specimen of an American alligator. He had all of his digits and appendages and his tail was full length, and Lester intended for him to remain that way — thus, the solitary confinement. There were probably bigger alligators in the communal large alligator pen, but all of these were scarred because of infighting or competition at feeding time.

There was another special alligator in the large pen. I had never been introduced to the animal and wasn't aware he was among the dozens in the pen. Some people that Bill Piper knew socially, or perhaps they were visiting relatives from Ohio or Michigan, came into the Gardens while I was guiding and he was giving them a rare personalized tour. They arrived at the pen just a few moments before my tour group and I walked up to it. I waited before I started to speak because I was interested in finding out what Bill was doing. I wanted to hear what he was saying.

The big alligators were in their usual relaxed mode and all was quiet. It was part of a guide's regular presentation to step over to the side of the pen, where Bill and his guests were gathered, to reach a pail filled with fish scraps that a staff member positioned when they heard me start the present tour. After I had concluded my discussion about alligators I would toss these goodies into the pen and the lazy-looking alligators would explode to life and the customers would be awed.

All of a sudden, Bill Piper spoke, "Blindman!" On the far side of the pen a large alligator turned its head, and Bill repeated the word, "Blindman!" The twelve-foot alligator started to move in Bill's direction, attracted by his voice. Bill called the animal by name again, "Blindman!" By now the alligator had moved across the pen, climbing over its captive cohorts and was now directly beneath Bill. Its head was close to the wall and Bill dropped a mullet head with backbone still attached beside the alligator's jaws. The instant it struck the water it was grabbed, precisely located by the unique sensory organs[26] that the crocodilians have. Then after another split second the fish head was crushed, the remains positioned, and Blindman swallowed them in one gulp. Bill dropped another few fish parts to the alligator and moved on.

After seeing this, I often did the same thing if I had a group of really interested people, to get some movement in the pit. It was surprising, because of the lack of motion, just how many visitors doubted that the alligators that were on display were actually alive. Movement by Blindman dispelled that notion and then, when I heaved a bucket of fish parts to them, that really brought the modern day dinosaurs to life. I was always amazed that when they heard the word, "Blindman!" every other alligator in the pen didn't respond and head to the source of that sound, expecting food, too.

The collection at Everglades Wonder Gardens also contained two enormous alligator snapping turtles. This species does not occur in the Everglades. Their natural range is the river systems of the Gulf States, but they do occur naturally in Florida north of the Suwannee River. Bill and Lester wanted to display specimens of the alligator snapping turtle because this species is the largest fresh water turtle in North America, and one of the largest forms among the fresh water turtles anywhere in the world. Specimens of these interesting giants would enhance the exhibition value of their permanent collection. It turned out that one of these individuals might have been among the largest specimens ever recorded for this species[27].

Most wildlife-based attractions in Florida exhibited small flocks of flamingos. To tourists these brightly colored birds epitomized and conveyed the tropicality of Florida. Although they were native to the state up until the nineteenth century, flamingos had been extirpated from Florida and in the early fifties the closest wild colony to Florida was in the southern Bahamas.

see the FAMOUS EVERGLADES WONDER GARDENS on U. S. Hwy. 41
In the Heart of the Everglades

Some of the Gardens' beautifully hued adult flamingos, circa 1956. The common condiment, paprika, was liberally mixed into their food to help sustain the bright adult plumage. This captive collection was widely known for its superb color.

Hialeah Race Track, in Miami, contained a large collection of these birds. Some of them were capable of flight and would occasionally fly out of the racetrack and temporarily disperse into the wild. Flamingos successfully reproduced at the Hialeah track and there were so many produced each year that the keepers could not capture and pinion[28] all of the young birds to render them flightless. Flamingos at roadside zoos, like Everglades Wonder Gardens, were purchased from wild animal dealers. That is until 1956, when Naples High School biology teacher Laymond Hardy gave Lester Piper some sound advice.

Laymond Hardy's suggestion was simple, "Lester, if you will drill small holes close together in a length of garden hose so it will seep and then keep it running to flood that corner of their yard, that will give the flamingos a source of mud from which they can build their nests. They can't do that without a large area of real soggy dirt. I'd also put tarps on the fence around that same area to give them a sense of privacy. If you'll do those two things you'll be able to produce your next generation of flamingos. You won't have to buy them anymore." Lester took Laymond's wise advice, and in short order the birds were scooping up mud and fashioning their unique tall conical nest platforms. They were soon laying and incubating eggs. The flamingo collection at Everglades Wonder Gardens became self-sustaining after 1956.

Among the publicly favored stars of the show were the river otters. The otters at Everglades Wonder Gardens were advertised as the "vagabonds of the swampland." These active animals were the last stop on a complete tour. After explaining the natural history of Florida otters, the guide would excuse himself and walk to the upright refrigerator in the slaughterhouse for a pan of cut mullet. Back at the pen, when the otters saw the guide rest the pan on the top of the wall, the animals came to life and went through their usual escapades of diving, twirling underwater, and then climbing to the unflooded part of the pen. They would line up and stand erect on their hindquarters, in anticipation of food. The guide would hold the fish and reach out with it and feign tossing it to get the animals performing. Most guides had scarred fingers because exuberant otters had jumped and nipped them when grabbing the fish — if it was held too close when the guide took a chance on hand-feeding them. It seemed this was a game the otters played

The author feeding the otters during a tour, in 1958. I'm wearing my brand new and expensive Stetson hat that Lester Piper had given me as a gift. In the late 1950s we employees wore blue uniforms, which the Gardens rented and were routinely laundered by the supplier.

and they intentionally bit the holder of the food. Most of us learned it was far safer to toss the food than try to hand-feed. Later, a child's fiberglass slide was installed in the otter pen. This gave the public another perspective of this animal's fun-loving and playful attitude.

The first otters to come into the collection were live-trapped by Bill Piper along the Peace River near Arcadia, in 1941. Bill visited the area for five days and sat motionless on the bank and carefully watched a family group playing near their den. The young otters, ever inquisitive, would occasionally stick their heads up above the riverbank to check him out. Bill noted their behavior and fully understood their daily routine before he selected the spots to set up his live traps. Over the years the Pipers reared many young otters and some of them became remarkably tame.

Chapter 10

The Crocodile Kings

THE EVERGLADES REGION'S WILDLIFE collection housed and displayed at the new Bonita Springs Reptile Gardens continued to grow daily. At first, the cages and pens were makeshift. Over time, as income from paid admissions increased, money became available for reinvestment and financed a variety of improvements and enlargement of facilities. People from the area continued to bring in orphaned wildlife to the Gardens and Bill and Lester Piper continued their snake-hunting expeditions into the Big Cypress Swamp and out into the Everglades. Frightened or concerned residents around Bonita Springs sometimes complained loud and long about nuisance alligators near their homes. The Pipers would respond, capture the problem alligator, and add it to their growing alligator collection. The brothers learned from commercial fisherman that American crocodiles had infrequently been observed in the Bonita Springs area in the past. These fishermen sold the Pipers fish for animal food, and after learning about the possibility of resident crocodiles, the brothers made a few nighttime excursions by boat down the Imperial River and into Estero Bay. In reality, these usually brackish water animals were very rare this far north on the coast of the Florida peninsula. The opportunity for Bill and Lester Piper to actually capture one never materialized until many years later. They wanted a specimen in their collection as a drawing card because few Americans knew that southern Florida was the only place on the planet that alligators and crocodiles sometimes lived side by side. So, they advertised and offered to buy any crocodiles that commercial fisherman anywhere in South Florida could capture for them. The message spread, mostly by word of mouth, and the cash-strapped commercial fishing community along both coasts of South Florida was abuzz. Before long the Pipers learned that all the crocodiles that lived in Florida Bay and the southern Everglades "belonged" to a tough Florida Cracker by the name of Argyle "Pigeye" Hendry. If they wanted to buy a crocodile they would have to deal with him, and he lived in Monroe County. His reputation was renowned; he was a hard-ass negotiator when it came to pricing live crocodiles.

In 1937, the Piper Brothers took a step toward special-ization, when they negotiated the purchase of an American crocodile from this crotchety old man who lived in a tiny tin shack, or sometimes aboard a dilapidated houseboat, at Rock Harbor on Key Largo. Like many other old timers in the Florida Keys, old man Hendry did not own an automobile. His sole mode of transportation was a small flat-bottomed boat that was powered by a temperamental one-cylinder inboard engine. He also owned a leaky Glades skiff he used to pull behind it to transport his gear and catch. Whenever he hunted crocodiles, the skiff was towed behind the powerboat and then poled into the shallows of the tidal red mangrove forest between Cape Sable and Key Largo. If Bill and Lester wanted a crocodile they would have to go to Key Largo and pick it up and pay folding money — cash on the barrelhead — and they soon learned the final price would be haggled over to the bitter end. For the next ten years they would buy every adult crocodile the old codger could catch for their exhibit,. This eventually amounted to fifty of the giants, and many smaller individuals.

The Pipers decided early on to advertise their crocodiles as Florida crocodiles, instead of using the proper name — American crocodile. Their play on words raised an element of curiosity to the traveling public and it proved to be an asset, increasing visitation. Tourists wanted to get a first-hand look at a genuine crocodile — in Florida they could see alligators any day of the week. It worked and they were soon featuring "Giant Florida Crocodiles" on their growing array of roadside white on red slat signs along the Tamiami Trail. Their simple outdoor advertising program was paying off.

Photo courtesy of Anna Piper Mackereth.

Lester (left) and Bill Piper, in 1954 — the American crocodile kings with their crocodiles.

The crocodile hunter was born William Argyle Hendry in 1869 in Polk County, Florida. He relocated to Dade County, where he married and then finally settled in Rock Harbor on Key Largo.

He bounced between his shack and his houseboat when he was not camped somewhere out in the Everglades hunting and fishing. He had a unique way of capturing crocodiles. After locating their den, a long tunnel the animals usually dug in a mangrove-lined tidal creek bank, he would decide whether the crocodilian was at home or out and about. If signs around the den's entrance convinced him the resident was inside he would take the wooden floorboards out of his boat and position them like a fence to block the entrance to the crocodile cave. Then he pulled his Glades boat up broadside and pushed it tight against the floorboards to give them added support and to strengthen the barricade, just in case the trapped crocodilian tried to escape by rushing and throwing its weight against the obstacle that blocked the entrance to its home. Hendry wanted to limit the possibility of the crocodile escaping from his makeshift corral, so he worked slowly and methodically. His next step involved taking a long steel bar and probing down into the mud every foot or so to track the hollowness beneath him and trace the alignment and direction of the submerged tunnel.

Once Argyle's probe rod contacted the resistance of tough crocodile hide, he knew the croc was positioned at the end of the tunnel. Argyle would then unload more steel rods from his skiff and drive them into the mud. These were driven several inches apart, through the soil and void, and then deeper into the soft bottom of the den cavity. They were inserted fully across the cave's width, but not far enough apart for the crocodile to pass through. The crocodile was now caged and escape was virtually impossible. The old man caught his breath for a few moments, and then took a sharp axe from his skiff and cleared away the vegetation above the underground spot where experience told him the crocodile was located. The next step was more labor intensive. He began to dig a hole through the ceiling of the den chamber. When his shovel broke through into the cave, the frightened crocodile became defensive and responded to the light with tooth-studded jaws apart and high-volume hissing. The trapped crocodile had by now turned and was positioned to face its adversary — a determined tobacco juice-spitting skinny man standing above it. The old man prepared a line and skillfully formed and dropped a series of half hitches around the toothy jaws, positioning them correctly with a pole and pulling them taut each time a hitch was in place and encircled the jaws. Soon the jaws were tightly secured together. Next he had to pull the very irritated shaking and rolling crocodile partly out of the cave and secure its front legs together at a point halfway over its back so that the front half of the beast was then incapacitated. The next step was to pull the crocodile further out and similarly tie the rear legs. Nearly exhausted at this point, Hendry would occasionally take a break to get his wind, before searching for a nearby reasonably straight mangrove limb. After he found and cut this from the tree and trimmed away its branches, he had a reasonably straight pole. Argyle's next step was to secure the crocodile's jaws to one end of the pole, and then, in sequence, tie the front and rear legs to the pole that he had aligned down the animals body length. The last stage of completely securing the croc for transport was to tug and pull it completely out of its den. Argyle Hendry, after considerable effort and having his legs slapped a few times by the powerful sideways flailing tail, eventually succeeded and had it tied tightly to the pole, too. The crocodile was now immobilized and could be safely dragged over the mud and loaded into the reassembled Glades boat. After all fastenings were inspected to insure they were tight, the exhausted crocodile hunter poled to his anchored motorboat for the return trip to his place on Key Largo.

Next to his home and dock at Rock Harbor, Argyle Hendry had built a simple stockade in the water. It was a fence made from poles that he had driven vertically into the mud and then tied together with rope at the top. This amounted to a strong pen that would hold any crocodiles until they were to be picked up. A narrow door in the wall of the stockade allowed access and after dragging the trussed crocodile inside, Hendry would skillfully untie his captive and release it into the enclosure. His next step would be to write a letter to Bill Piper and advise him that another crocodile was ready to be picked up. He usually also informed Bill as to the animal's sex and length in his crudely composed hand-written in pencil letters. Bill then planned a road trip to Key Largo a few days later to pick up the prize and notified Hendry of the date by mail. A typical Hendry letter, the only one remaining in Bill Piper's daughter's collection of her father's papers, is simply composed:

Lake Supriz Fish Camp
Rock Harbour PO Fla

Feb 7 — 1940

Dear Mr Piper.
I examined the crock to day
Find it is a female.
I am kepin on hunting now and
I am shure that I get you a mail
In a few days now
Ill let you no as soon
As I git on yurs

Very Risp.

W. A Hendry

Bill Piper then told Lester and Frances that he was headed for Key Largo on a certain day to take delivery of another crocodile. Whenever it worked out with his young sidekick's school schedule, Bill asked Donald Trew along to keep him company on the trip. If this couldn't be scheduled because Donald had other obligations, he would take along someone else he knew for company. These trips were usually two or three day excursions. They would have their gear packed and leave Bonita Springs early in the morning in Bill's General Motors panel truck, but their initial destination was not Key Largo — they were headed first for Coral Gables where the Whittles still lived.

The marriage of Bill and Frances Piper had been steadily deteriorating and both were becoming unhappy in their marital relationship. Bill had had his eye on Alida Whittle for some time and it was always evident to a third party that from her obvious flirting and teasing demeanor, she was after him, too. Bill and Alida managed to accommodate one another and be together whenever the opportunity arose and by now they had an established romantic routine. By 1941, this relationship became more serious and Bill and Frances' marriage began to fall apart further. Bill would drop Donald at the Whittle family's place where he would visit and socialize with the younger Whittle children while Bill and

Alida slipped away and went out on the town. Bill and Alida would return by sunup, Donald would be rousted and dragged out of bed, and he and Bill would head down U.S. Highway 1 for an early arrival at the Hendry place on Key Largo.

Argyle Hendry always respected Bill and addressed him as "Mister Piper," both in one-on-one conversation and in correspondence. However, the wise, mean-spirited, old Cracker always managed to out-fumble Bill and finagle the top dollar out of him for one of "his" crocodiles. A seven-foot crocodile would fetch Argyle $50.00 in 1940, but the bigger they were the more cash money he expected. Once Bill inspected a crocodile and found it in good condition, the bidding war started and the price escalated as Hendry stubbornly refused to accept each amount Bill offered. Each time one of his oral offers was summarily rejected by the old codger, an aggravated Bill would utter, "The hell you say!" and quickly make another. Crocodile hunting was the old man's primary source of income and his exclusive livelihood, although when younger he occasionally supplemented his income by hunting alligators for their hides, like many of his younger Gladesman cohorts. Another enterprise of his consisted of robbing crocodile eggs from the nests that he found on the small mangrove keys of upper Florida Bay and selling the hatchlings to tourists and the Miami pet trade as "baby alligators." Many of Argyle's crocodiles ended up in household aquariums in the north. Argyle Hendry knew from experience when Bill's offers were reaching their maximum limit, and after a lot of complaining and excuses and cussing the old man would cave in and accept Bill's top dollar offer. Inflation had entered the American crocodile market, and as the years passed, with each negotiated sale the prices climbed. When the prices that Bill paid for crocodiles back in the late thirties are compared to the value of a dollar today, the amounts he paid Hendry for crocodiles do not sound substantially excessive. However, in those days, the purchases amounted to a tidy sum. On July 22, 1939, Bill picked up one ten-foot female crocodile, one eight-foot female crocodile, and four-dozen crocodile eggs and paid Argyle Hendry a total of $80.00. Today, this purchase price would be equivalent to an expenditure of about $1,300.00.

Bill and Argyle recaptured and trussed the crocodile, tying it to a long board that Bill had brought along. This time the tightly secured crocodile was blindfolded and then loaded into the panel truck. Donald Trew remembers times that a few specimens were so long that even though their heads were positioned as far forward as they could be shoved, to a point between the front seats, the tails still extended so far back beyond the vehicle that when the doors were tied closed the crocodile tails extended beyond them.

Even though the crocodile was now loaded in the vehicle and they were ready to roll toward home, Bill and Donald weren't completely free from crafty Argyle Hendry. As far as the old man was concerned, anytime that Bill Piper bought a crocodile, he was committed to drive the crocodile seller up to a Homestead grocery store and then back home again — a fifty-mile round trip — before Bill could strike out for Bonita Springs. With each newfound money supply, Hendry invariably bought a large box of staple groceries, and a full carton of Apple Sun-Cured Thick Cut Plug Tobacco. He quickly opened the large carton and pulled out and unwrapped a plug, but Argyle was unable to bite it off because of dental problems. So, he pulled out his well-honed pocketknife, cut a huge chunk from the rock-hard plug, and shoved it into his snaggletooth mouth. On the way back to Key Largo, Donald got to sit between the two men so Argyle could spit the juice from his wad out the passenger window into the breeze.

Before Bill and Lester unloaded the dry crocodile and carried it to its new home, Bill would always inspect the passenger side of his vehicle to see how much of Argyle Hendry's tobacco juice had splattered on the truck's body and stained it. Invariably it was well-spotted and streaked. Bill would gruffly say to Donald, or whoever else had ridden along with him on the trip, "Get a hose and clean that shit off."

At the Bonita Springs Reptile Gardens, the crocodile was released into an expanded facility. By 1941, two large concrete-based flooded enclosures had been designed and built to accommodate the growing collection of adult alligators and crocodiles. Like many of the Gardens' other smaller enclosures, vertical wood boards formed a wall to contain the collection. Both "pens" would later be enclosed with replacement masonry walls.

The alligator pen would eventually be enclosed with surplus silo blocks that Lester had acquired, and a concrete block wall would retain the crocodiles. Both would later have top-mounted, inward angled, steel welded-wire fencing added to prevent human arms and legs from being extended down into the pens or out over the walls.

Argyle Hendry continued to catch American crocodiles for the Piper brothers until 1947. He also occasionally led museum and university expeditions from as far away as Milwaukee, Wisconsin, on their quest for crocodiles. Over the years he supplied a number of specimens to America's largest zoological parks. Through the years the Piper brothers remained his best customer, until the American crocodile finally became protected in Monroe County after the establishment of Everglades National Park, in 1947. The crocodiles of Florida Bay no longer "belonged" to Argyle Hendry but to the people of Florida and the United States of America. Argyle Hendry quietly passed away in 1954 with tobacco-stained spittle draining from his smiling mouth — American crocodiles were probably his last earthly thought.

Alfred Trew stayed with the Pipers until after the outbreak of World War II. He decided he would leave Bonita Springs and join the U.S. Merchant Marine. He left town in 1942. During the war Alfred shipped out of both east and west coast ports and served on ships that plied the Atlantic and Pacific Oceans. In 1945, he returned to Bonita Springs to visit his family and the Pipers. He found Frances to be very unhappy and the two of them decided that when he left town he would take her with him. They did leave together, and Alfred gave Frances the attention and support that she deserved.

The couple struck out first for Miami, where Frances quickly filed for a divorce from Bill Piper. This was final in a relatively short time because Bill didn't contest it. He wanted the marriage ended so they both could move on with their lives. Following the recording of her divorce, Frances and Alfred married and soon departed Miami by train for the Detroit area. They remained there for a time and decided that their new life should really begin in the far west, in San Francisco, California. Before they made that move, Bill sent Frances a quitclaim deed for her to execute. She did, and Bill was free to sell their former Orange Street home in Wyandotte. He was burning his bridges, and his former wife and her new spouse soon boarded a train for the "Golden State."

At about the same time the Trews were speeding west for a new life in California, forty-five-year old Bill Piper was speeding east across the Tamiami Trail — he was headed for Coral Gables and the arms of thirty-one-year old Alida Jane Whittle. Bill popped the question that she had been waiting for a few years to hear, and Alida agreed to marry him. They returned to Bonita Springs and were married in Saint Xavier Catholic Church in Fort Myers on June 19, 1945, by the Parish Priest, Vincent Crawford. Since Bill's first marriage had not been performed under the purview of the Church, it was not considered to be legitimate by doctrines of the Roman Catholic Church. His divorce was also not worthy of consideration according to Church policy and the couple were given permission to marry in the Church. Alida's new in-laws, Lester and Lucille Piper, were not entirely thrilled when Bill remarried.

Chapter 11

The Competitive Edge

IN 1938, A CANADIAN couple named Harold and Mildred Crant invested in some prime real estate in Bonita Springs. They had wintered in the town for a few years before buying the four corner parcels where Terry Street intersects with the Tamiami Trail. This crossroads was about an eighth of a mile north of where the entrance of the Bonita Springs Reptile Gardens was located. The Crants built, stocked, and opened a commercial enterprise on the parcel on the northwest corner. They named their tourist-oriented business The Shell Factory. This quickly grew into a multi-building complex where seashell products like lamps and curios and souvenirs were manufactured on site. A large showroom was dedicated to the retail and wholesale sales of seashells, seashell-based products, and other marine collectables.

The Shell Factory employed many people who lived in Bonita Springs, Estero, and Fort Myers and a company-owned bus transported the contingent of workers to and from Estero and Fort Myers to their Shell Factory jobs in Bonita Springs. Harold Crant launched a major outdoor advertising campaign and his billboards extended all the way north to the Georgia border, along all major highways. These included both U.S. 41 and U.S. 301. In the day these were the major arterial highways that tourists would travel to connect with the section of U.S. 41 known as the Tamiami Trail and pass through Bonita Springs. Their ultimate destination was usually the over-rated and crowded Miami. Billboards also dotted the northern edge of the Trail, directing tourists who were traveling north to his establishment as they drove west from Miami. The landscape along State Road 80, the east west aligned highway that crossed Florida connecting West Palm Beach to Fort Myers, was also included in this vigorous pre-television advertising program to attract travelers to The Shell Factory. In short order The Shell Factory became a lucrative enterprise as tourists flocked to it. The Crants next expanded and built the Dome Restaurant across the highway from the Shell Factory on the northeast corner of the intersection. This unique building was designed to look like the top half of an orange. It was circular and had a round roof that was painted bright orange. The citrus fruit motif was complete in detail, having a green stem and leaves connected to it at the very top.

Lester Piper soon considered the competition from the Crants as a serious financial threat and he quickly gravitated toward disliking Harold Crant. He was convinced that The Shell Factory, and even the Thomas Edison Winter Home in Fort Myers (which had opened to the public in 1947) redirected or short-circuited potential tourist dollars that would have otherwise been expended at his Gardens had the close competition not been implemented. His opinion did not effect Lester's long term and very cordial, friendly relationship with Bob Halgrim[29], the manager of the Edison Winter Home.

Harold Crant was an entrepreneur and Lester really got bent out of shape when Crant brought in a few families of Miccosukee Indians and set up an attraction cater-cornered from The Shell Factory (on the southeast corner of the Terry Street and Trail intersection) and named it Distant Drums. Undoubtedly, the business' name was a take-off from the 1951 Florida-based movie of the same name. This enterprise was complete with chickees, where the resident Indians actually lived and worked. Years earlier, Ross Allen had included an actual Seminole Indian village as part of his operation at Silver Springs. Distant Drums provided tourists a living visualization of the Florida Native American lifestyle and offered their primitive colorful handicrafts for sale. The Distant

Drums village was also complete with a live alligator wrestling show. Lester Piper became more irate when the Crant operation started to exhibit the alligators. He took it as a personal affront that Harold Crant had the gall to advertise and display alligators within two hundred fifty yards of the Gardens — almost directly on Lester's doorstep. Lester Piper never said it out loud, but he was most likely delighted when The Shell Factory complex burned to the ground on New Year's Eve, 1952. The Crant family left Bonita Springs thereafter and rebuilt The Shell Factory in North Fort Myers, where it remains open for business[30] today.

The Piper brothers struck a bump in the road early in 1946, when reports reached the Florida governor's office that wildlife exhibits around the state were fronts for illegal gambling operations. He then instructed sheriffs throughout the state to "check up on skin games at so-called 'wild animal and snake shows.'" Governor Millard Caldwell claimed he was concerned that these exhibits "may be a front for an insidious gambling racket," and launched the statewide investigation. In a press statement issued January 31, 1946, the governor implied that the Everglades Reptile Gardens[31] was included among those reputed facilities tied to gambling. Bill Piper moved to counter the allegations and denied any connection to the rackets. He and Lester sent a joint telegram to the governor, insisting they were not associated in any way with the illegal gaming industry. The contents of this telegram were printed in the Fort Myers News-Press on February 2, 1946.

The telegram article raised some public interest and the popular News-Press "In the Mailbag" column published a letter to the editor written by John R. Jack, Jr. a few days later that connected Everglades Reptile Gardens to gambling. In his letter Mr. Jack wrote, "It was not necessary for Mr. Piper to visit any snake show to understand the gambling operations, as a reference to the court records in Lee County, for the winter season of 1940-41 and 1941-42 will show that in each of those years men were arrested, tried and convicted of operating gambling devices in his snake show. Seems the officials were doing a pretty good job."

Bill and Lester retaliated and paid for and published the following letter in the News-Press on February 3, 1946:

An Open Letter to Gov. Caldwell

Dear Sir: I note in yesterday's paper that you have asked all Florida sheriffs to check up on operations of so-called snake shows, presumably including the one we operate at Bonita Springs.

I have the honor to advise your exellency that the Everglades Reptile Gardens, which we have managed since 1937, is no front "for an insidious gambling racket," as the statement you issued from Tallahassee would imply.

Ours is a strictly reputable enterprise, as are those of such educational exhibits as Dr. Marshall Bishop's near Miami, E. Ross Allen of Silver Springs, Thompson's Wild Animal Show at St. Petersburg, Michel's[1] Reptile and Animal Farm of Sarasota, the North Miami Zoo of Miami and others throughout the state.

As you very well know, Governor, authorities in certain counties have been induced by bribery and other corrupt means to permit the operation of gambling in their counties, of which racketeers posing as wild life experts constitute only one phase.

You well know — as do your subordinates — who are the guilty officers of the law. Why then, do you not take action against them, dismiss them from office and see that they are brought to justice?

Instead why do you chose to cover your own negligence in enforcing the laws of the State of Florida by broadcasting a wholesale libel against honest and honorable men engaged in providing an interesting and legitimate attraction for tourists, as well as our own citizens?

> Yours very truly,
> BILL PIPER
> LESTER T. PIPER
> Everglades Reptile Gardens
> Bonita Springs, Florida

[1] Correctly spelled Mitchell.

The issue soon drifted off into obscurity after this short public exchange. Bill and Lester were never charged with participating in any gambling or shill scams. In 2009, I talked with Alfred

Trew about this era and the gambling question. He told me, "Some of their old cronies from Detroit came to Bonita Springs in the wintertime and set up a Three-Card Monte game in the back of the Gardens, to fool around and have something to do. They used playing cards and someone turned them in to the sheriff up in Fort Myers. He came down and ran the guys off. The Pipers were trying to get away from that old lifestyle and had nothing to do with the card game. They weren't paying attention to what their buddies were doing."

Bill and Lester built and opened their own restaurant in 1949. This was probably done in a retaliatory move to compete with the Crant's The Dome Restaurant. Their eating establishment, The Garden Inn, was located close to the Gardens' entrance and also fronted on the Trail. It became a popular eatery and visitors often dined there before or after their visit to the Gardens.

As time passed, other wildlife attractions began to spring up in Florida. The Florida Wild Animal and Reptile Ranch opened in Saint Petersburg in 1937, the year after the Piper's operation opened, and it lasted for over twenty years before closing in 1959. Gatorland in Kissimmee and the Miami Serpentarium both opened their doors in 1948, and Gatorama opened on U.S. 27, south of Palmdale, in 1957. Of these three, only the Miami Serpentarium[32] is no longer open to the public. Slowly the Piper brothers were being nearly encircled by competition as others who were also interested in making money invested in their own tourist-supported roadside zoos.

In 1955, a Charlotte County entrepreneur opened a wildlife exhibit and named it "Everglades Wildlife Park." This new attraction was located on the west side of the Tamiami Trail on the south side of Punta Gorda. Those of us around him on the day he learned the news knew that Lester Piper was noticeably upset about the new wildlife operation in the neighborhood. He showed us the entire article about the new attraction's grand opening that appeared in the Fort Myers News-Press. Lester admitted that he was especially angry because it had been given a name so close to that of his own wildlife exhibit, and it was obvious to him why. We could always tell when Lester was in one of his bad moods. He didn't announce it, but he would always send clear and easily read signals that he was worked up about something. It was like an audible alarm whenever he was tossing metal feed pans about and they were bouncing around and making a racket at the beginning of the workday. Everyone around him went about his business until Lester calmed down. This had been one of those mornings.

Lester knew he would be recognized if he visited the new attraction himself, and he was seething inside for a description of the new competitor's exhibit. What might they be displaying that Lester didn't have in his collection? Lester asked me if I would go there as his surrogate — as his spy. He came right to the point and asked, "Charlie, when you have time will you go up to Punta Gorda and check this new place out for me? I'd like to know what the hell he has and how he's got the place laid out." I told him I'd check it out as soon as I could on one of my days off. I wouldn't be in a rush to go there because he didn't offer to give me any compensation for doing his detective work.

When I decided to make the trip and visit Everglades Wildlife Park I enlisted a friend to go along with me on this undercover operation. "Sonny" Marine and I went in the entrance building and paid our fee to go inside to see the exhibits. Unlike the Wonder Gardens, this place had no guide to explain things and we were left entirely on our own to wander the grounds. Things started out without a hitch, but I made the mistake of periodically taking a small memo pad and pencil out of my pocket and noting things that we saw. Someone must have seen me taking notes. By the time we were about half way through the exhibits, an angry old man suddenly confronted us and yelled that he was the owner. He demanded to know what we were doing? Then he stared at me for a few moments, and said, "I recognize you . . . you work for Bill Piper! Did he send you up here to spy on me? I want you both to get the hell out of here . . . right now and don't ever come back! Get!" The old buzzard didn't even offer us a refund. We stopped at the Gardens and I reported the events of the day to Lester. He thought the whole escapade was hilarious, and didn't even offer to reimburse us for what we had spent to get in the place as his undercover investigators. Everglades Wildlife Park made it for a few years but closed soon after the owner died. It never seemed to be much competition for Everglades Wonder Gardens.

Later in 1955, another ominous cloud rose over the future of Everglades Wonder Gardens when the Florida Department of Transportation announced plans to reroute the Tamiami Trail to the west of downtown Bonita Springs. The town was going to be bypassed. Lester was depressed when the news was released because he knew that without traffic flow his operation would be far more negatively impacted than what the effect of some upstart competitor might cause. By the time the right of way for the new four-lane highway was cleared, Lester had already discussed some of his concerns with a few close acquaintances. He feared that after the Trail was rerouted future attendance at the Gardens would drop off. Stephen Briggs, of Outboard Marine Corporation, offered the Pipers a tract of land on the southwest corner of the intersection of the Tamiami Trail and State Road 29 at Carnestown, the Everglades City junction. Briggs dabbled in wildlife movie making and made frequent visits to the Gardens to briefly film birds, but the main purpose of his visits was to record audio of certain species to be later added to his nature film's sound tracks.

Lester and Bill mulled over this offer. There were many positives to the idea of relocating Everglades Wonder Gardens. Certainly, the location was excellent because of traffic flow. Lester figured that because of the potential site's location it was doubtful that even the stupidest of the state road department's bureaucrats would conceive a plan to realign the Tamiami Trail near Carnestown. The size of the offered parcel would provide a better and roomier layout. Lester would be able to build larger quarters for his collection and enable him to develop a design more in keeping with the modern habitat displays that were coming into vogue in the larger zoological parks in America. After procrastinating for a time, the Piper brothers eventually decided to decline Steven Briggs' offer. They would remain in Bonita Springs.

In 1955, a group of investors approached Bill and Lester. They wanted to purchase a forty-acre parcel of land owned by the brothers. This tract was located near the corner of the Trail and an unpaved trail that later would become an eastern extension of Bonita Beach Road. Another forty-acre parcel was situated between the desired parcel and the Trail, and the prospective buyers wanted a deeded easement through it to the forty acres they were interested in buying. This land was all part of the Piper brothers' Bonita Springs pasture that straddled the Collier and Lee County line. Bill and Lester were receptive to the sale and the financiers made a substantial offer on the parcel, pending the outcome of decisions by Lee County and the State of Florida. The would-be buyers made the sale conditional on the political entities approving a zoning change and approving their application for a greyhound-racing track. When word got out that the would-be purchasers were going to build a dog track, it split the community of Bonita Springs down the middle. Some ranted and raved about the evils gambling would bring to their community while more progressive citizens saw a dog track as a boon to employment opportunities and a boost for the local economy. The Piper family saw a future dog track bringing more visitors to Everglades Wonder Gardens, and the agreed-to price for the acreage was nothing to slink away from in 1956. In the end, the pro-dog track people won out, and everything went well as the issues passed through the state and county hoops and permits and licenses were granted for a greyhound track. The Pipers sold the property to the Bonita-Fort Myers Corporation on November 19, 1956, and the Naples-Fort Myers Kennel Club opened in late 1957.

After rumors had circulated for a couple of years, big time competition impacted Everglades Wonder Gardens on September 1, 1969, when Ohioans "Jungle Larry" and "Safari Jane" Tetzlaff opened Jungle Larry's Safari at Caribbean Gardens in Naples — just sixteen miles down the Trail from the Piper brothers' attraction. The Tetzlaffs had relocated most of their large collection of wildlife to Naples after discovering the beautiful tropical gardens that were owned by Julius Fleischmann. When Fleischmann was approached initially he had no interest in bringing the Tetzlaff operation to Naples, but, shortly after, when he passed away, those managing his estate saw the wildlife exhibit as a good addition to the gardens that Julius Fleischmann had nurtured and financially supported with his millions. The Tetzlaff's relocated to Caribbean Gardens[33].

Years later, Interstate 75 created another major bypass and directed even more traffic away from Bonita Springs. Mega attractions like Disney World, Sea World, and Busch Gardens opened in Central Florida and the remaining small privately owned wildlife attractions began to close their doors. Bill and Lester had turned down some offers for Everglades Wonder Gardens made by potential buyers in the 1950s. In the 1970s they declined a substantial and serious offer to purchase the Gardens that was tendered by one of their employees. Later the brothers expressed a willingness to negotiate a deal with Lee County. The county was developing Lakes Regional Park on the corner of the Tamiami Trail and Gladiolus Drive and someone suggested that a county-owned zoological park, which could have been based on the Piper collection to start, be located on this property. Lee County Commissioners failed to recognize the opportunity and the Pipers withdrew their offer to negotiate with the county. The people of Lee County lost out again because of poorly performing County Commissioners.

Chapter 12

The Movies

WHENEVER MAJOR MOTION PICTURE studios, making adventure movies selected Florida for a filmmaking location they usually wanted footage that included graphically violent human and native wildlife confrontations. These shoots often included shorts; brief films that were filed away until needed and then added into any number of future films of the same genre. Violent scenes of large alligators supposedly interacting with human victims were always incorporated in a Florida-based production if they were in any way connected to wild Florida. Advance men for the movie companies discovered and singled out the Piper brothers as a supplier of animal actors. When location shooting was scheduled, the Pipers were contracted to supply those live animals necessary for the production. Lester continued to prefer the background and Bill Piper was usually the one who would be hired as an animal handler. Some of the scenes included in the shorts for which they supplied animals were later edited into outdoor-oriented movies, such as the popular Tarzan series.

The first major motion picture production the Pipers were involved in was the Technicolor film, *The Yearling*. Marjorie Kinnan Rawlings wrote this literary masterpiece, in 1938. It was adapted into a screenplay by Paul Osborn and filmed on location in

1946 in Ocala National Forest at a place now known as the Juniper Prairie Wilderness. The film was released by Metro-Goldwyn-Mayer in May of 1947. Clarence Brown directed the film which starred Gregory Peck, Jane Wyman, and Claude Jarman, Jr. *The Yearling* won a variety of awards including the Academy Award for Best Art Direction-Interior Decoration, Color, and Best Cinematography, Color. Gregory Peck was nominated for Best Actor in a Leading Role, and Jane Wyman for Best Actress in a Leading Role. Because of his youth Claude Jarman, Jr. was awarded a special Oscar for his performance. Others received nominations for Best Director and Best Film Editing. *The Yearling* was also nominated for Best Picture.

Up and coming actors Forrest Tucker and Chill Wills had roles in *The Yearling*. Other actors who were completely unknown at the time, like June Lockhart, had minor parts and were not included in film credits this early in their careers. Bill Piper received no credit for his work in *The Yearling* either, although his favorite bear became a major animal star when he performed above and beyond.

Bill Piper's connection to *The Yearling* began years earlier, back in 1941, when a man came into the Piper brothers' Everglades Reptile Gardens on February 25 and offered to sell them three very young, quite recently born Florida black bear cubs. In the late 1930s Bill and Lester had decided to change the name of their wildlife attraction, thinking that the word "Everglades" would boost visitation, and it seemed to. The person who presented the little bears in a gunny sack claimed that he had found the orphaned cubs out in the Big Cypress, to the south of Bonita Springs in Collier County at a place known at "Rattlesnake Hammock." He told Bill that he had found the cubs floating on a log, but because the bears were so small, the Pipers doubted his tale. They suspected this guy had killed the cubs' mother after he had discovered her den. They asked no further questions after considering the alternative fate that might befall the cute cubs if they didn't make the purchase. Bill quickly negotiated a $45.00 buying price for the trio. He paid the man — thinking, "This guy is in no way was as shrewd as Argyle Hendry. Argyle would have gotten into a bidding war with me and would have demanded a lot more cash." The triplet bear cubs were given the names "Tom," "Dick," and "Harry." They were a handful and the chore of raising them on a nursing bottle was delegated to Frances Piper. When they weren't gulping formula their constant playmate was young David, Lester and Lucille Piper's son. David could play just as hard and rough as the bears demanded.

David T. Piper, Sr., 1941, with Tom, Dick, and Harriet at play on the grounds of the Everglades Reptile Gardens.

When they were large enough to no longer require constant care the cubs were collared. During daylight hours the trio were often chained in the yard to interact with employees and sometimes patrons, under the careful supervision of the Garden's guide. As the bears grew someone on the staff happened to notice that it would be more appropriate to change Harry's name to Harriet. Tom and Bill Piper bonded, and as long as Bill passed the bear an occasional open bottle of Pepsi-Cola with a rubber nipple in lieu of a metal cap their relationship was acceptable and amenable to the bear. Pepsi-Cola was the soft drink of choice for bear treats because, after all, the company's slogan of the age told why: "Pepsi-Cola hits the spot — Twelve full ounces, that's a lot — Twice as much for a nickel, too — Pepsi-Cola is the drink for you." Bill Piper was known to sometimes be a "penny pincher," and the "twice as much for a nickel" part sold him on the product.

Tom, like all bears in captivity, could be very sneaky at times and one didn't want to have a finger anywhere near the wire when the bear was active and pacing back and forth at the front of his cage. An example of what Tom could do unexpectedly was the time the Florida Game and Freshwater Fish Commission wanted to use the bear for a short film that would be shot as part of an educational package on which they were working. Bill trucked the bear to a prepared caged site near Arcadia. Upon his arrival at the filming location he called on a few wildlife officers who were standing around to help him unload the portable cage from the trailer. One of these men had a finger that could not be bent and when he grabbed hold to help with the cage his stiff finger stuck through the wire into Tom's space. It was quickly amputated by Tom's bite. According to David Piper during a 2009 interview, "Old Tom just sucked the damn thing right off."

When it came time for the trip up to the Ocala area to shoot Tom's part for *The Yearling*, one of the movie executives telephoned Bill and asked if he had any dogs that could be used in the bear chase scene he wanted to include as part of the project. Dogs that have no fear of bears — canines who are tough and wily enough to engage an adult black bear, are few and far between. Bill told him that he himself had an untested dog when it came to bears, but he was sure his dog would at least give a loud chase to the bear.

He was not sure if he would actually fight the bear. He told the producer that the best bear dog he knew about was one owned by a Florida wildlife officer who was a friend of his and lived nearby in Naples. Bill was told the studio would hire the officer's dog and the producer asked him to contact his friend and make him a monetary offer for the use of his dog. Bill contacted Luby Kirkland[34], the bear dog's owner, and arranged to borrow the animal on behalf of the movie studio. Bill would take the animal along with his dog and Tom up to Ocala when the outdoor set was ready and filming of the bear scenes was scheduled.

This particular dog was one very tough and highly prized animal. He wouldn't hesitate to confront and fight bears, panthers, or feral hogs. He wasn't a personable human-connected, friendly pooch and was considered by those who knew him . . . knew enough to keep their distance . . . as a mean dog. The animal had been around Bill Piper enough times that he tolerated him — complete strangers had better steer clear. Luby Kirkland's dog's genealogy included a variety of mixed-breeds that were specially and purposely bred from what originally was predominantly based on bull terrier stock. These powerful dogs were commonly called Florida cur dogs, and the demeanor of their mean-tempered pit bull ancestry usually showed up.

The film crew was ready and had selected a location for shooting the highly anticipated bear scene. Tom the bear would transition and become "Old Slewfoot," the marauding black bear made infamous by the book, *The Yearling*. Bill Piper and Luby Kirkland's dogs would be used in this and the other bear chase and fight scenes. They would play the parts of "Julie" and "Rip." The movie workers had erected a temporary high chain link fence and formed a long compound in which the bear chase scenes would be shot. The fenced area was wide enough so that the fence was hidden from the camera lenses by thick natural vegetation around the inside perimeter of the compound. Several cameras were set up along the length of the flooded raceway to catch the action.

After Tom's cage was positioned at a small opening in the fence, Bill stepped out into the far end of the compound with a bottle of Pepsi-Cola in his hand. At the director's call, "Action!" Bill raised the bottle of Pepsi and called out, "C'mon, Tom!" When

Tom heard Bill's voice and glimpsed the bottle, the bear had all the direction he needed and he charged out of the cage door when it was opened. He raced through the water and headed for Bill and the bottle. At the same time, Bill began to run back, aiming for his exit point through a doorway at the far end of the compound.

Photo courtesy of Anna Piper Mackereth.

Tom the bear and Bill Piper on *The Yearling* set, 1946. Tom was five years old at this time. Note the heavy leather jacket Bill is wearing for upper body protection should something go wrong, and the wire fencing behind them to prevent Tom's escape..

This, like the other bear scenes, was to be shot in only one take, so everyone associated with the shoot had to be at the top of their game. Everyone performed well except Bill Piper. When Bill saw that Tom had been released and was scrambling in his direction Bill started high-tailing it for his escape hatch. Suddenly, he slipped on the partly flooded ground and fell, landing spread-eagled and nearly face down in the mud.

Tom was coming on strong and Bill feared that when the black missile got to him he was going to end up severely injured if not outright killed by the charging movie star. For some inexplicable reason, when Tom reached Bill, who was still prostrate, he ran over him without stopping. The cameramen had captured a great bear run, but when the film was processed, they learned that all of them had missed the action of Bill falling and the bear running over him. The running footage was a take.

The next scenes were shot over several days and were a combination of short runs by Tom with the dogs at his heels and the dogs cornering and fighting the bear. This footage turned out to be one of the best and most realistic dog and black bear fight scenes ever filmed . . . because it was real. However, it turned out to be realistically deadly for Luby Kirkland's prize dog. Rip would not retreat and did not dodge away in time and Tom caught him in his powerful paws and mortally bit the dog breaking the animal's neck. The dog had to be euthanized. Several cameras had captured the death grip and it remained in the final cut of the film. In 1946, movie credits were just beginning to add a statement regarding the care of animals during filming to announce to viewers that no animals were mistreated or injured during filming. The following statement appears at the end of *The Yearling*:

> All scenes involving animals in this picture were made under the supervision and with the cooperation of the American Humane Association.

The dog's death was unintended and an unexpected event that just sometimes happens when wild animals are involved in movie making.

In compensation for his dog's demise because of the power of Old Slewfoot, above the agreed-to animal acting fee Luby

Kirkland's wife, Lozzie, was awarded a brand-new gasoline-powered Maytag washing machine. This would be the first mechanical washing machine the Kirkland family had ever owned and the days of washtubs and washboards were over for Lozzie Kirkland.

When *The Yearling* was released Tom the bear became an overnight national celebrity. The Pipers quickly capitalized on the public's mood and changed their outdoor advertising. Their refurbished, homemade, slat signs had a new message to inform motorists that their collection contained Old Slewfoot of *The Yearling* fame. Visitation at Everglades Reptile Gardens skyrocketed. The Gardens became a must-see destination not only for tourists from all over the country but also Florida residents who could make a visit to see the famous bear as part of a family day trip.

In the late forties, Bill and Lester changed their exhibit's name again, this time to Everglades Wonder Gardens. The name change seemed to increase visitation and it was their opinion that the use of the word "reptile" had caused many visitors, especially women, to shirk away from stopping because the mere word reptiles implied snakes.

In 1950, Hollywood-based Republic Pictures Corporation approached the Piper brothers. Their film crew was planning to visit Florida to film another adventure movie to be titled *Distant Drums*. The storyline of this film was roughly based on the Seminole War of the 1830s. Gary Cooper, Richard Webb, and Mari Aldon were the major stars and Raoul Walsh would direct the movie. It would be filmed at several Florida locations including Castillo de San Marcos in Saint Augustine, Turner River near Ochopee, in a borrow canal along the Tamiami Trail, the beach of Keewaydin Island (south of Naples), and accessible areas of the Big Cypress Swamp close to Naples. Many residents of Bonita Springs and Naples were hired to assist in production of the movie. Some worked on the sets on location, others were stand-ins or were brightly painted and played the parts of Seminole Indians.

Distant Drums, a Technicolor production, was released on December 29, 1951. There is neither a trail of paper nor cinematic

credit evidence that substantiates the oft-repeated story around
Bonita Springs that Bill Piper was a stand-in for Gary Cooper in the
action scene where the Cooper character comes riding into the set
on horseback after the trek to reach Army headquarters. It certainly
looks from the rider's physical appearance like it could be Bill
Piper on the horse. Incidental to this production Bill and Lester
supplied a panther, some snakes, and a few alligators. Footage
sequences of these animals were filmed and then inserted into the
movie during final cutting and editing. There is no credit given on
the film or in any available records for either the animals or a
possible stunt or stand-in role by Bill for Gary Cooper. They
certainly were much alike in stature and it could have happened.

Hollywood had discovered the Piper brothers as a source
for Florida wildlife when such was needed for on-location filming.
Finally, in 1953, they got their big break, the opportunity to appear
on the big screen during the filming of United Artists Corporation's
Florida color adventure, *Shark River*. This movie was shot in and
around the Hole-in-the-Wall cypress strand near Naples and was
directed by John Rollins. The film's primary actors were Steve
Cochran, Carole Mathews, and Warren Stevens. Bill Piper is
included on the film's credits as an actor along with Robert
Cunningham, Spencer Fox, and Ruth Foreman. His name is also on
the lobby cards that were circulated to theaters that were showing
the film.

Not long into the movie, a full-bearded Bill Piper comes
galloping onto the screen. Florida wildlife officer Ray Barnes
flanks Bill on his right and his brother Lester is to his left. All three
men are seated on horseback. Bill is playing the part of a sheriff
who is leading a posse in the first few minutes of the movie. Bill
speaks two lines of dialog. After he and his posse take some
potshots at the fleeing felons, Bill spits and says, "The fool. Boys,
this is as far as we need to go."

Earlier in this particular story line Don Carroll, an
Everglades Wonder Gardens employee, also has a speaking part as
he fills the role of a deputy sheriff. First, his voice is heard off
screen as he utters, "Raise 'em high!" As he enters the scene Don
is knocked to the ground by one of the bad guys, and when

questioned as to where his horse is, he replies, "Behind the house." This film has countless scenes that include wildlife species that were supplied by the Pipers.

The next motion picture in the Piper's movie portfolio was *Yellowneck*. This was a low budget, poor quality color film that was shot in 1954 and released by United Artists Corporation March 22, 1955. The director of *Yellowneck* was R. John Hugh and the film's stars were Lin McCarthy, Steven Courtleigh, and Berry Kroeger. As the credits roll at the start of the film the following statement appears on the screen:

> All scenes in the heart of the Florida Everglades were accomplished only through the kind cooperation of the Seminole Indians and Bill and Lester Piper of the Everglades Wonder Gardens.

In 1958, Warner Brothers crews came to Southwest Florida and changed the appearance of Everglades City. They were trying to duplicate what Miami looked like around the beginning of the twentieth century for a movie set for their production, *Wind Across the Everglades,* scheduled for filming in and around Everglades City. The movie's theme was a take on the battle between plume bird hunters and Audubon Society wardens during a time when a growing public outcry demanded that the wanton killing of egrets and herons for their feathers for the millinery trade be halted. Nicholas Ray directed the movie and big name stars were Burl Ives, Christopher Plummer, and Gypsy Rose Lee. The actor's credits name three locals who were part of the cast. The father and daughter team of Corey and Mary Osceola had prominent speaking parts and did an excellent job. This was Peter Falk's first movie and the Osceolas had stronger roles than he. Chokoloskee Island resident "Totch" Brown appeared and was also included in the credits. Animal footage included species that were rented from Everglades Wonder Gardens, but the Pipers and their attraction are not included in the film's credits. During their stay in the area many of the actors and Warner Brothers staff associated with the movie project were frequent visitors to Everglades Wonder Gardens.

Color versions of *The Yearling*, and *Distant Drums*, and a black and white issue of *Yellowneck* were released and made available in both VHS and DVD formats. *Shark River* has been released in VHS only, and at the time of writing, *Wind Across the Everglades* has not been released by Warner Brothers in either media. Pirated copies, taped off television presentations of the film, have gone for significant amounts on eBay. There is hope that *Wind Across the Everglades* will be available on DVD soon, since the studio is now releasing more obscure films on DVD from their library through the new online Warner Archives division.

Chapter 13

When Panthers Ruled

SOMETIME IN THE LATE THIRTIES someone found a Florida panther kitten out in the Big Cypress, not too far east of Bonita Springs. It was not unusual for panthers to be observed around the town, and in 1937, resident Mitt McSwain shot and killed one not too far from the Bonita Springs Cemetery. The tiny spotted cat was brought to the Pipers and was quickly purchased and added to their collection. Its mother had probably fallen victim to a hunter, but the kitten was so small its eyes were still closed and it needed almost constant attention. This survivor could only have been found if the finder or his dogs had stumbled on its mother's birthing den or happened upon her while she may have been moving her litter. Lucille Piper took over the responsibility of hand-raising the kitten and Lester named his wife's tiny feline ward, "Queen."

Queen became exceptionally tame and remained attached to Lester for all of her long lifetime. Lester collared her so she could be controlled with a leash when they often strolled around the yard of the Gardens. A new cage was built for her and she settled into a long life of captivity. Whenever this cat saw Lester, she immediately broke into a cadence of loud purring and vigorously rubbed her agile body against the wire of the front of her cage. At the very sight of Lester, or the sound of his voice, Queen exuded total affection. This beautiful cat would become the queen mother of Lester Piper's Florida panther collection.

Lester Piper, circa 1946, with his wild-caught Florida panther, Queen (left) and her grown captive-bred kitten, Kitty.

A couple of years later this story repeated itself when an orphaned male Florida panther was brought to Everglades Reptile Gardens. This cat was several weeks older than Queen had been when she was caught, so there was no serious attempt to tame the feisty male cat, although it had to be nursed with a bottle. It was given the name of "Tom." Tom's origins had also been the wilderness out to the east of Bonita Springs. The state of Florida was paying bounties on this native cat during this period, and therein lies the reason for the frequency with which orphaned Florida panthers reached the Pipers. Tom soon grew into a very large handsome adult. He was by far the largest example of a Florida panther to ever enter the Piper collection and he would live long and lead a sexually active life.

When Queen and Tom matured, Lester decided he would attempt to captive breed these fine cats. By 1942, he had developed the methodology and increased the cage space to hold cats that were produced in house. Slowly over the years the collection grew. Sometime in the mid forties someone who had a male Costa Rican cougar that they were unable to keep presented the cat to Lester. Lester Piper always found it difficult to refuse animals that needed care[35]. During this foreign cat's time at the Gardens it was housed solitarily in a cage at the rear of the yard, located between Tom the panther's cage and Tom the black bear's cage. This cat never left this cage from day one, nor was a Florida panther ever introduced into the cougar's cage. Anyone with basic observational skills could see that this animal was much different than the Florida panthers. It was a different color and had a smaller body size, but the most remarkable difference was in its legs. One could plainly see this stocky appearing feline had extremely short legs compared to those of the native Florida subspecies. That this cat was even housed in Lester Piper's panther collection would erroneously cloud the genealogical origins of his cats almost two decades later.

Queen's third litter produced a fine pair of male kittens. These were stunning and perfect examples of the Florida panther and were hand-raised by Lester and Lucille. Lester found that, unlike females, these male cats could become rambunctious. Their play was very rough. After they matured they were retained together in the same cage that was located near the otter pen. Lester would occasionally go inside with them and they would play exuberantly with him. On one occasion one of the cats pounced on Lester from behind and the animal's sharp claws raked his upper back. Lester's visits inside the cage became more infrequent after that experience and when he did go inside to interact with the cats he donned a heavy leather jacket that was kept hanging on a hook next to the door of the cage. The first few times he wore it inside their cage the panther twins weren't too happy — the strange odor of the leather baffled them. These male panthers became poster cats for some of the major advertising for Everglades Wonder

Gardens. A photograph of them together was used on a brochure cover, a popular black and white postcard, and even on a souvenir pennant[36].

Lester would continue to captive breed his panthers but not at the potential pace he could have if encouraged. There was no need to do so because wild-caught panther kittens continued to be brought to the Gardens. In 1953, two wild-caught Florida panther kittens were brought to the Gardens from a ranch near Devil's Garden in nearby Hendry County. A couple of years later, in 1955, a cattleman acquaintance of Bill Piper brought in a litter of three from near Sunniland, out in the Big Cypress in Collier County. Their eyes were still closed and Lucille Piper had her hands full raising three active kittens at one time. I personally was on hand when both of these litters arrived at Everglades Wonder Gardens.

In 1956, Marlin Perkins, director of the Lincoln Park Zoo in Chicago, Illinois, shipped Lester an adult western cougar as a gift. This cat was surplus to the zoo's needs. Marlin thought it was a courteous gesture on his part, to repay Bill and Lester for the many kindnesses they extended to Marlin Perkins' snake collecting expedition that had visited Southwest Florida, in 1955. Like the Costa Rican cougar this cat was never put in contact with a female Florida panther. I can state this unequivocally because I was on staff at the time and I was privy to every attempt at panther breeding between 1953 and 1957, and throughout 1958. I physically helped move cats around. The only panther cage that was connected by a doorway with another cage was one that had an attached den box. When the female cat in this cage was receptive, in heat, the door between her cage and Tom's cage was opened to allow contact. Without a doubt, during the fifties the integrity of the Everglades Wonder Gardens' Florida panther gene pool or bloodline was indeed sustained by cats either bred in-house as a result of selective pairing and mating between Florida cats, or exclusively with cats that had been wild-caught and admitted to the collection. Meanwhile, the bounty system for panthers in Florida had been eliminated. In their unprecedented wisdom, the Florida Game and Freshwater Fish Commission began to assess the remaining Florida panther population and finally admitted that because of their failed management and hunting policies, the

Florida panther would soon become extinct in Florida unless something was done.   That same year, the Game Commission began inspecting and increasing their administrative control over zoological parks and the few remaining roadside zoos like the Piper brothers' operation.

A new cadre of wildlife biologists were recruited by the Florida Game and Freshwater Fish Commission. Overnight these people were transformed into Florida panther biologists — or as Lester Piper used to chide, "They're wonder boys with a little book-learning who wear shiny shoes that they're afraid to get muddy or wet." Earlier, most of the new hires didn't even know that the Florida panther existed, and for sure they had never observed a Florida panther in the wild, nor were they familiar with the Big Cypress where the remaining Florida panthers were making their last stand. They had to rely on others for their expertise. These experts didn't have a clue as to the history of the Florida panthers that resided at Everglades Wonder Gardens, so they did like so many others of their profession have always done; they made assumptions.

Counterparts on the federal level soon joined these panther biologists as concern rose for the survival of the Florida panther. They started to develop recovery protocols for the cat not long after the Florida panther was first designated as endangered in 1967. Funding for the planning effort for the cat's recovery increased when the Florida panther was listed as endangered under provisions of the federal Endangered Species Act, in 1973. The question of the bloodline of the Pipers' captive animals was raised and soon became an issue among the members of the Florida Panther Recovery Team. Purportedly, testing of some of the few Florida panthers that were remaining in Everglades National Park indicated that the examined cats from the Park were not genetically pure Florida panthers. Rather than blame the release of some unrelated cat into the Park by one of the many keepers of captive cougars in South Florida, they attacked the Piper collection. They suggested that Lester Piper had introduced a non-native cat into his breeding program — a preposterous continuance of an assumption. It never happened and the biologists had wholly fabricated that contemptuous suggestion. It is true, however, that with considerable media fanfare, a pair of surplus purebred Florida panthers from the Wonder Gardens was accepted by the National Park Service and released into the Park in the mid-fifties[37]. An online literature search suggests that up to seven individual panthers from the Everglades Wonder Gardens were purportedly released into Everglades National Park. Lester Piper was a poor record keeper, and left no paper trail. If five more of his panthers were indeed released into the Park, the releases occurred after 1959, and I seriously question the documentation. As recently as 1973, a letter from the Superintendent of Everglades National Park encouraged Lester Piper to release more captive-bred panthers there.

Photo courtesy of Bob Garrison.

An adult male Florida panther produced at Everglades Wonder Gardens being released into Everglades National Park, in 1956.

The recovery team appointed for the Florida panther tripped up and stumbled when they started to implement their recovery strategies for the cat. They failed to encourage Lester Piper to breed more of his cats for release under their recovery plan.

Finally, they came up with the idea to have hunters capture a number of female Texas cougars, bring them to Florida, collar them for telemetry tracking, and release them into the Big Cypress to breed with resident cats. The Texas cats were taxonomically related to the Florida cats, but they were not as genetically close to the remaining wild stock as those captives housed at Everglades Wonder Gardens. The wonder boys were determined to completely sidestep the fact that pureblood Florida panthers were caged in Bonita Springs. It would have taken just a little push for Lester Piper to be enlisted and breed his panthers to assist the survivorship of this big cat in Florida.

It's true that Lester Piper had developed somewhat of a grudge against the Florida Game and Freshwater Fish Commission and he had just cause for doing so. In 1956, the agency was filming a series of short films on various species of Florida wildlife, the rare panther among them. Earle Frye, the assistant director of the agency, and Bill Piper were friendly. Earle asked if the Pipers would furnish the loan of a panther for this moviemaking effort. Bill agreed but Lester wasn't too happy because he knew who would have to make an extra effort. Tom and the twin males were out of the question and the breeding female was an expectant mother. This left only "Kitty." Kitty was from Queen's first generation of kittens, and like her mother she had been hand-reared and was very affectionate toward Lester. Lester boxed her and some Florida wildlife officers showed up on schedule to transport the cat to the film set's location, a beautiful Spanish-moss draped cypress setting near Fisheating Creek. During the filming Kitty's leg was somehow broken and the cat had to be euthanized. Lester was upset for days after and he never forgave the Florida Game and Freshwater Fish Commission for Kitty's injury and untimely death.

The pedigrees of Lester Piper's Florida panthers were never compromised. The aberrant bloodline that is said to exist in the panthers of Everglades National Park may indeed be due to a release there by an unknown party. Wherever the animal responsible for the genetic contamination came from, it did not originate in Bonita Springs.

Tom was the only panther used as a stud for years and was the father of several litters. His rein as head panther ended when he had to be put down, in 1958. I would see the outwardly tough and grizzly Lester Piper burst into tears twice in the forty years I knew him. The second time was when he had just euthanized Tom the panther after the old cat's kidneys had failed. Like the first time, I would join Lester in tears. Following Tom's death, every two years thereafter Lester would move one of two sibling male Florida panthers that were caged adjacent to the otter pen into the cage of the female he was using as a breeder in the rear cages when she was receptive. From the available newspaper evidence it appears that the last time Lester hand-reared a panther from among Queen's lineage was in 1974.

Of interest is a letter that Lester received, dated May 13, 1985, from Robert Baudy of The Rare Feline Breeding Center near Bushnell, Florida. In his letter Baudy mentions an approaching panther meeting in Tallahassee and he queries Lester about his original Florida panther stock. He begins, "In view of the fact that you were the only people to receive animals from the wilds[38] . . .." He goes on to ask five questions about the physical characteristics of Lester's original panthers and to seek information on the releases of his cats into Everglades National Park. Lester turned this letter over to Bill[39] for his attention. Bill was 85 years of age, and I doubt there was ever a reply issued. Only the original letter from Baudy remains among Bill's papers. Again, the wonder boys were a day late and a dollar short and stubbornly continued to steer their Florida panther recovery program based on junk science.

Chapter 14

Old Slewfoot's Retirement Years

BILL PIPER WAS A tall man. In his prime he stood six-foot, two-inches tall and when he coaxed Tom the bear to stand erect on his hind legs beside him, while he raised a cold Pepsi, the huge bruin stood every bit of six-feet tall — a large male Florida black bear. Bill fully respected the power of Tom and the inherent danger he exposed himself and others to when working with this animal outside of a cage. At the same time he had convinced himself they were buddies and Tom was completely under his control. When invited, Bill even dared to take his bear along to nearby cities to participate in public celebrations. Tom would have a chain leash attached to his collar and they would stroll along the parade route together. One of the keys to such outings was to have an assistant nearby with an inexhaustible supply of Pepsi Cola or other treats Tom enjoyed. The complete trust came to an end in the late forties, not too long after *The Yearling* was filmed, when Bill Piper made an innocent blunder to which the bear reacted.

Tom was quick on the draw when it came to emptying a Pepsi bottle. He soon realized that when he was getting close to emptying the soda bottle that if he bit off the nipple he could completely drain all of the sweet fluid in one last hurried gulp. Bill didn't care for this new trick and he decided the next time it happened he would pull the bottle away from Tom's mouth before he could bite completely through the rubber and drain the bottle. The next time it happened Bill was ready and did exactly as he had planned. Tom was not a very happy black bear. The bear became immediately enraged and promptly attacked and grabbed Bill with a combination of claws and teeth and knocked him down. After his blows sent Bill to the ground, Tom seemed to totally lose interest in what he had done — lucky for Bill Piper. The bear looked around, as if trying to decide what his next move would be, and he noticed the inviting open door of his nearby cage. Tom, completely ignoring Bill, ambled over to the opening and returned to his comfort zone. Bill was bleeding profusely, but managed to get to his feet and closed and locked the cage door behind Tom. Lester drove his injured brother to Lee Memorial Hospital, twenty-three miles away in Fort Myers, for medical attention. It took twenty-seven stitches to repair the damage to Bill's throat and shoulders. This mauling deterred Bill from taking Tom out of his cage anymore and he no longer took him for the occasional walk around the yard, or for a photo opportunity requested by visiting media.

After this near-death experience, during an interview[40] Bill Piper said, "Florida has many bold bear hunters and trainers — but Florida has no old, bold bear hunters and trainers. Florida black bears have a one-track mind and a poker face. No matter how docile and friendly they might appear, they're constantly dreaming of the day when they have gained your full confidence. That's the day they'll try to grab and kill you."

The Pipers learned a lesson from Bill's experience and adopted a new personal safety policy. Before either of them interacted with a bear or a panther in the future they donned heavy leather jackets to protect their bodies and extremities should such an event ever occur again.

After Tom had injured him, Bill Piper ended his close-up interactions with the bear. It had been a close call and Bill didn't wish to repeat the incident or experience worse because the bear was now growing temperamental and untrustworthy. Old Slewfoot would continue to be the center of attention for many visitors to Everglades Wonder Gardens. In 1955, the Naples Drive-In Theater in North Naples booked *The Yearling* for a special showing and arranged with Lester for the bear movie star to be exhibited at the theater. David Piper and I towed a trailer with Tom's cage down to the drive-in so he would be present and the center of attention for the evening. Because of good advance press coverage the event was well attended and people crowded around the cage to see and hear about Tom. This would be Tom the bear's — Old Slewfoot's — last public outing.

Over the years many Florida black bears became part of the Gardens' wildlife collection. Some would be raised to adulthood and released, returned to the Big Cypress Swamp to fend on their own. On August 6, 1955, Bill released a three hundred-pound male bear named "Smokey" out at Corkscrew Swamp to join two females he and Lester had turned loose there earlier in the year. The bear collection at Everglades Wonder Gardens was now down to three, Tom (Slewfoot), "Bonnie," and "Donnie."

Only so many bears could be part of the permanent collection since space was limited. The few bears that were obtained young enough and were considered special because of their size or temperament remained captives. All were small cubs when they were brought in and sold to the attraction, supposedly orphans that had been found by people who were residents of communities in the Big Cypress region, or individuals who regularly hunted there. Bears were never among the limited number of captive-bred wildlife species successfully propagated by the Piper brothers. All of their bears were wild-caught.

Other than Tom, a female black bear named "Suzie" was considered mild-mannered and special. She was a charming and sometimes manageable resident early in the days before Tom, Dick, and Harriet arrived on the scene. Bill and Frances Piper put a lot of care and affection in raising the cub. As she matured, Bill would often chain Susie to a post and interact with her for the customers, but he finally realized that this was an accident waiting to happen and stopped the practice. Up until the time Susie was nearly full-grown Alfred Trew would take the bear from her cage, attach a chain to her collar, and lead Susie down to the edge of the Imperial River for a swim. The bear enjoyed bathing in the water and Alfred admitted seventy years later that it was sometimes difficult to get her to follow him back to her cage because she enjoyed the water so much.

One bear in particular, no one remembers the animal's name, caused some apprehensive moments for Bill and Lester in the early days. An experienced employee of the Gardens was routinely assigned the job of feeding the bears at a prescribed hour. Their daily diet was a generous helping of a mixture of oranges and water-dampened dog kibbles[41]. These were mixed with bone meal and vitamins and served in a large round, flat metal pan. The pan was supposed to be placed in the cage by sliding it through a long clean-out flap that was hinged and extended completely along the front of the very bottom of the cage. It was on July 17, 1951, when for some reason known only to him, this worker decided that on this particular day he had become a skilled bear trainer. He placed the food pan directly in the cage by opening the main door instead of doing what he was supposed to do. When he swung the door open, the bear decided it was time to make a jailbreak. She rushed the opening and forcibly made her way past the keeper, knocking him aside with a few blows that left bloody but superficial scratches on his upper body. These were inflicted when she pushed the astonished animal keeper completely out of her way. Of course, as one can expect, Murphy's Law applied to this situation and the bear ran directly toward the main building and the door through which customers entered the yard after being told inside which way to go to catch up with the guide and join the tour group. At about the time the bear reached the door, it opened and out stepped a gentleman and his son. The teenager, sixteen-year old Richard Neumann, from Hamilton, Ohio, was in the lead. The frantic keeper hollered for them to get back inside the building for their safety, but they didn't heed the warning, apparently transfixed by the sight of the loose bear charging toward them. The bear plowed into the boy and bit him on the neck after she bowled him to the concrete. The lad was extremely lucky the bear didn't bite harder or severely maul him. The wannabe bear trainer was still in pursuit and screaming at the top of his lungs for Bill and Lester. The boy's father, Richard, and another spectator jammed a stick in the bear's jaws. Bill heard the entire racket and came running to see what the hullabaloo was about. He grabbed the bear by the ear and twisted it. The bear released the boy and Bill tempted the animal back into its cage with a loaf of bread.

The injured teenager was rushed to Lee Memorial Hospital in Fort Myers. Although the boy's injuries appeared to be nothing more than shallow tooth punctures the Pipers feared the youth's neck and bone could have been damaged internally. According to David Piper, who was present during this episode, the father of the boy was ranting that he wanted the name of a lawyer and threatening a lawsuit. In good faith and in an attempt to avert this from happening, Bill and Lester went to the hospital and paid all of the boy's medical costs. As far as anyone can remember the Gardens was not sued over this incident.

In late 1954 the screwworm fly was a very serious threat to wildlife and livestock in Florida. The slightest open wound provided an access point and the flies deposited their eggs on the margins of any fresh wound, however minute, on the skin of mammals. These eggs quickly hatched, some in but a half-day and the maggots that were produced were soon mining into living tissue, consuming the flesh as they bored in. Newborn fawns and calves were highly susceptible to infestation at their fresh, still open, umbilical scars, and, if left untreated, their flesh would be eaten away during the screwworm flies life cycle. The infested animal would waste away and die. The enlarging gory wounds would continue to be a depository for a steady onslaught by adult screwworm flies and their eggs and the resultant larvae used the living food source for their development until the animal died.

Tom's cage was in a long block of multiple cages on the back of the yard and next to that of a younger male Florida black bear, named Donnie. They were separated from one another by a steel chain-link partition. Habitually, whenever one of them was close to the wire, the other one would try to bite him. In late 1955, Donnie succeeded in nipping off the very tip of Tom's ear when he noticed it was protruding through the wire into his territory while the older bear snoozed. No one on the staff noticed the wound at first. The next morning on one of my earliest guided tours I happened to see groups of tiny white screwworm fly eggs that had been deposited and had adhered to the fur near the bleeding raw periphery of the bite. By the time I noticed the eggs, some of the larvae had likely hatched and were already burrowing deep into the top of Tom's ear and voraciously consuming the live tissue. I told Lester and he inspected the bear's ear through the wire. He tried to wash away the eggs from the ear with direct pressure from a hose but Tom didn't appreciate that very much and withdrew to the rear of the cage out of range of the direct spray. Something had to be done soon.

The next day Bill came into the Gardens and he must have told Lester he wanted me to help him treat Tom. I was temporarily relieved from my guiding duties and my relief guide directed me to meet Bill at Tom's cage. Bill held a full Pepsi-Cola bottle with a large nipple affixed to it and a small cardboard carton. He explained to me that he was going to put Tom out and then he and I were going into the cage to manually remove all the screwworm maggots in the tissue of the bear's ear. We would also remove the mass of necrotic tissue from the wound, remove any additional fly eggs that had recently been deposited around the wound site, and then seal the site to prevent any further reinfestation.

I stood in front of the cage watching the bear pace back and forth while Bill went around to the rear of the cage and unlocked and opened the door about half-way. He called Tom and the big bear walked over to him. Bill talked to him soothingly then passed Tom the Pepsi bottle. The bear sat down on his haunches and lifted the liquid goody to his lips. Tom bit the nipple off cleanly and gulped his soda. He then lowered the bottle and lost his grip on it. The bottle struck the concrete floor without breaking. Tom again began to slowly pace the cage and after about ten minutes his movement slowed and he seemed to stagger — five minutes more and the bear was out cold. Bill told me to come around to the back and follow him into the cage. I did, at the same time hoping the sedated bear didn't awaken. I knelt down on the hard cement across the sleeping bear's head from where Bill was kneeling. This was happening before the introduction of tranquilizer-filled darts that are so commonly used today in wildlife veterinary work. I was curious so I asked Bill what he had used to knock Tom out? He replied, "I gave him a Mickey Finn." It did the trick and the bear was sound asleep.

Bill passed me a flashlight from the box and told me to hold it and illuminate the wound. The cage was partially shaded and Bill had to have light to see to work. On closer examination I could now see that most of the top and one upper edge of Tom's ear, most of the helix, had already disappeared — eaten away by the hungry maggots. The wound which led into the thinly separated inner tissue of the helix had a terrible smell when I leaned even closer to watch as Bill began to clean the area with a water-soaked rag. After most of the rotten fleshy material was wiped away the remainder had to be cut away with surgical scissors and a scalpel. The maggots were now visible. Every so often Bill would tell me to move or tilt the bear's head so he could see from different angles as he searched for screwworm maggots. When he saw one, Bill took the tweezers and one by one pulled the resisting screwworm larvae free of their tunnel. Each, and there were at least two-dozen of the fat maggots, were over a half-inch in length. Bill probed and carefully inspected each empty tunnel to be sure he had removed them all. Next out of the box came a bottle of alcohol, which he liberally worked into and completely soaked the hole in the ear and then swabbed it dry with another clean rag. The final step involved application of a black, thick, tar-like substance that was in a small bottle. He forced this material down into the gaping wound with a wooden tongue depressor. Bill built this up liberally on the outside of the ear because he knew that when Tom came around he would try to both shake and scratch the substance out of his ear.

It only took this one treatment and over the next few weeks the bear's ear healed. Entomologists were actively working on a way of getting rid of screwworms with a new technique of gamma-radiating male screwworm flies to render them sterile. The concept worked and by 1959 the screwworm was successfully eradicated from the Southeastern United States.

After Tom's retirement, the large wire cage that the bear usually occupied when he traveled to a location for a film shoot was stored at the Wonder Gardens[42]. In 1954, the organizers of the Annual Swamp Buggy Days festivities down the Trail in Naples borrowed the cage to use it as a "jail." It was mandated by the organizers of Swamp Buggy Days that, during a declared period of time prior to the festivities, all the men in town must grow a beard or be locked up in the jail during the celebration. Clean-shaven men would have to pay a "fine" by purchasing a swamp buggy badge and then wearing it. If he were already wearing a badge a man could escape being "arrested" on sight. Without a badge you were locked up, and before you could be released you were publicly displayed in the jail along with your fellow "convicts." The jail was on a trailer and paraded down Fifth Avenue during the Swamp Buggy Parade. A recent book[43] about the history of this long-standing Naples tradition contains the following paragraph about the cage's loan. "Lester and Bill Piper, owners of the Everglades Wonder Gardens in Bonita Springs, agreed to lend Swamp Buggy Inc. Tom's bear cage for a swamp buggy jail. The Florida black bear's illustrious reputation preceded him all his life. He played Slew Foot [*sic*] in the movie "*The Yearling*[44]." The following year, in 1955, the author states, "The Bush Patrol thanked the Piper brothers for the use of old Tom's cage and built its own (jail) this year. Many beardless visitors and residents toured Naples from the inside of Tom's cage."

Later in this book, the writer mentions, "The man who lent the Bush Patrol his bear cage for its first jail in 1954 was honored this year (1978). Lester Piper, co-founder and co-owner of the Everglades Wonder Gardens received the Fourth Annual Bonita Springs Chamber of Commerce Citizen of the Year Award. Piper was an active member of the Bonita (Springs) Chamber which he, his brother Bill Piper and George H. Pochlmann, Jr. founded in 1953."

Tom the Florida black bear died suddenly at sixteen years of age in 1957, but Old Slewfoot the movie star lived on for a few more years. To take advantage of the advertising value of having Old Slewfoot on display, Lester quietly moved Donnie into Tom's former cage where the sign identifying Old Slewfoot of *The Yearling* fame still hung. Donnie grew to be a slightly larger adult than Tom, but only those persons who knew about the partially missing ear could tell the difference and knew Donnie was an imposter.

Chapter 15

Guitars and Gators Don't Mix

BILL AND LESTER PIPER had grown up enjoying what later became known as country and western music. Bill learned how to play the guitar during his stint in the Navy, and somewhere along the line he must have convinced Lester to pick up a mandolin and learn the instrument. The Piper brothers enlisted a few other musicians and formed a small band that played around Detroit, Michigan, in the 1920s and into the early thirties. His personal songbook from that era still exists. In 1932, Bill could often be found playing with a local group in the bar and grille that served as a community center at Doc Baird's campground in Bonita Springs. This building became a popular watering hole for a couple of generations of the town's thirsty residents and during the winter months its clientele of patrons swelled.

When Bill and Lester finally settled in as permanent residents of Bonita Springs, they were usually part of the local entertainment at Doc Baird's on Friday and Saturday nights. The brothers had been accepted by the townspeople as part of the community after they began showing what hard-working men they were as they began to improve their riverfront property. Bill and Lester generally came across as being tough guys, guys you didn't want to aggravate, as bits and pieces about their criminal past began to leak out into the community. From start to finish, their reputations maintained this aura among the people of Bonita Springs and Southwest Florida. Many residents disliked the attitudes of most of the seasonal northern visitors — the damned Yankees — who infiltrated their town's population, especially when northerners became dominant in the wintertime. After a few too many rounds of beer some townspeople reveled in picking fights with newcomers, especially over good-looking women who may have accompanied their husbands, or otherwise fun-loving ladies who dared come into the tavern on their own to dance. It wasn't at all uncommon for fights to break out between locals and tourists before the end of a night of dancing and drinking at Baird's place. It was sometimes a downright unsafe spot to be when fists started flying. The Piper brothers weren't exempt from run-ins and they had their share of scraps. Bill finally started to carry personal protection. According to Donald Trew it was common to see him stop after work, enter the small butcher room at the Gardens and pick up a sheathed skinning knife, before walking over to Baird's with his cased guitar . He would jam it into his belt and pull the tails of his shirt down outside his waist to conceal the weapon. Fights could get violent at Baird's at times, but Bill Piper never had to use anything other than his fists to protect himself or those with him.

Lester Piper couldn't dance, so his interaction with the ladies on a social level at Baird's was limited. He envied those of his peers who could dance, especially those of his friends who often got chest to chest with the big-busted woman who operated the Bonita Court Restaurant in the two-story building directly across the Trail from the Gardens' entrance. Rumor had it that Lester was interested in getting a grip on Margaret Myers out on the dance floor. He decided to quietly take some dance instructions and enrolled at a Fort Myers dance studio as a student. He kept his dance course quiet and, as a cover, he usually dragged Alfred Trew along with him into town on the nights he had dance class. Alfred was told to keep the reason for their weekly trips to town quiet. Lucille Piper was preoccupied raising her son David. She wasn't part of the community's social loop on Friday and Saturday nights, so Lester was free to play music and occasionally practice his dance steps at Baird's joint.

Bill Piper, in Bonita Springs, on December 23, 1934, strumming his 1933 Martin C-3 arch top guitar.

From all accounts, Bill was a very good rhythm guitar player with a mediocre voice. In the early thirties he played an expensive flattop Gibson guitar and in 1934 one of his favorite instruments was a 1933 Martin C-3. The latter was an upper end arch top model made by America's premier acoustic guitar-maker, the C.F. Martin and Company, Inc.

Bill's guitar playing came to an abrupt halt in 1950, because of an on-the-job accident. Animal bites and related injuries were commonplace for anyone in the wild animal business and the brothers had learned that early. By now, both of them had been seriously snake bitten and mauled by bears and panthers a few times, but each had been lucky because all of their body parts were yet intact. This physical perfection ended because of an alligator — an alligator that wasn't even part of the permanent collection at Everglades Wonder Gardens. Bill Piper was the victim and the story is best recounted in his own words. The following dialog was transcribed in its entirety from a video clip I filmed at Everglades Wonder Gardens on February 22, 1986. Bill and Lester had just finished holding a couple of year and a half-old, twenty-four-inch alligators for the camera when Ralph Curtis jokingly said to Bill, "The one that took your thumb off wasn't much bigger than that." Lester spoke up, "He was about seven or eight feet long." Then Lester tried to remember the incident, wondering aloud where the alligator that did the damage to his brother's right thumb had come from. He suggested that it had happened when they where getting ready to load some alligators to take them to the Southwest Florida Fair in Fort Myers. Bill then spoke up, "No, no. That was the gators that come from down on the Trail they took away from the Indians. And, they brought them up here and wanted to know if I'd take care of them . . . we did. They finally got a place to put them and the Game Department brought Harvey Douglas here and Luby Kirkland, they were both game wardens, to help tie these gators up. We were down to the twenty-fourth one — they had a bunch of them. I had his feet tied behind his back . . . he was lying there with his mouth open and I pushed his head shut. When I did my hand slipped off of him and he came back. Whew! Round and round. I said . . . I said, 'Harvey,' I said, 'He's got my thumb.' He said, 'Oh my.' He was holding the rope out, holding taut on it and he dropped it and ran. I couldn't do nothing. The doctor asked me, 'Where's the thumb?' I told him, 'Damned if I know. I took my pocketknife — it was just hanging there and I cut it off and threw it in the grass.' He said, 'If you had brought it up here we probably could have put it back on.'"

Bill could no longer hold a guitar pick between his thumb and forefinger properly and opted not to finger strum his guitar. From all accounts Bill Piper never played guitar again.

Chapter 16
The King Crocodiles

THE MATURE CROCODILE COLLECTION at Everglades Wonder Gardens was at its peak in 1955, and it was truly impressive to see so many adult American crocodiles in one group. Several males in the collection approached, if not exceeded, the maximum recorded size for this species in North America. Two huge males were at least fifteen-feet in overall length. Florida crocodiles are actually the same species that occurs through the larger Caribbean Islands and is found in all Central American nations and the northern countries of mainland South American. Florida is the northern periphery of this species' Atlantic Ocean range. Three other species of crocodiles occur in the lower latitudes of the same area, and some of these occur in the same habitats as the American crocodile. These are the Cuban crocodile, which is found only on the island of Cuba and the nearby Island of Youth, the Morellet's crocodile, which occurs in Southern Mexico, Guatemala, and Belize, and the Orinoco crocodile which is found in Venezuela and Colombia.

Warren Boutchia had a bad experience in the crocodile pen in 1953. He shares the following account, "My scariest episode during the time I worked with Lester Piper happened inside the large concrete pen that at the time held about thirty-five adult

American crocodiles. A section of concrete from the usually submerged pool sidewall that slanted to the bottom of the pen had cracked, and over time it had gone unnoticed. Water leaking through the crack had undermined the fill behind the concrete and the whole section had broken and collapsed during the night. All of the water in the pen had seeped out through the opening and the crocodiles were found to be high and dry in the morning. So, the entire Gardens crew pitched in and got repairs underway. After we drove the crocodiles back by poking them or knocking them on the head with long poles, we had to refill and pack fill dirt into the void and then mix and pour concrete. After the new concrete slab was poured and finished and all of our gear removed, Lester told me to stay in the pen and keep the crocodiles away with a long, wooden pole. I was to stay there as long as it took for the concrete to set-up. He told me, 'I don't care if you have to stay in here all goddammed day, I don't want them getting on the concrete!' It was clear to me that Lester didn't want the crocodiles to get on his repair and mark it up. Why, I don't know, because it was going to be underwater and wouldn't show. I guess he was just proud of his workmanship in finishing concrete.

"It so happened that the dominant male crocodile in the pen was a fifteen-foot-long brute that Lester had named "Ironhead." His snout was much broader than that of the usual American crocodile. His head was almost alligator-like, wide and rounded and he had an overall menacing appearance. He was tough, too. I watched helplessly once while he disemboweled a smaller crocodile before any of us could grab a pole and hop up on the wall to try and break up the fight.

"I knew it was going to be a long day so I took a book about wild cats with me into the pen to pass the time while the cement set. Every so often, I'd glance up from reading, and have to get up and tap some croc on the snout with the pole a few times to make it back off, trying to keep them at the far end of the pen and away from the wet concrete and me. This continued through the day, while I waited for the cement to harden to a point the crocs wouldn't damage the finish. I was really into the book and at the moment not paying too much attention to what was going on around me, when all of a sudden the hair on the back of my head felt funny — it was literally standing up. I glanced up, focused, and looked into the glaring brown eyes of Ironhead. He was only inches away and standing up on all fours. The bull croc with the bad reputation had quietly sneaked up on me and was staring at me with his mouth partly open, all of his ivory-white teeth fully exposed. If he had chosen to lunge he could easily have caught me and that would have been it. I reacted instantly and pushed myself away to get out of range. After gaining my feet, I slammed his head with the heavy pole to divert his attention, and then I scampered up the ladder that led out of the pen to reach safety. After a while I calmed down and went back to my station, confronted Ironhead, and drove him back again with the pole.

"Not too long after that day, Lester decided to isolate Ironhead because he was becoming too aggressive with the other large male crocodile that Lester had dubbed "Dynamite." He was a tough guy, too, but Ironhead was determined, hoping to out-compete Dynamite for domination of the collection, but he lost out because of his looks. Dynamite was a much more handsome specimen of an American crocodile so he got to stay in the pen and on exhibit — Ironhead would be the one to go. We roped and hauled Ironhead into a smaller adjoining enclosure not long after my scary experience. The last time I saw him, many years later when I made a trip to the Wonder Gardens to visit Lester, Ironhead was still in solitary confinement and out of regular public viewing. To this day, over fifty years later, I still get chills when I think about that close call."

The crocodiles were always my personal favorites. In 1955, the Gardens undoubtedly had the largest collection of American crocodiles anywhere — for that matter it was very possible that the Everglades Wonder Gardens collection held more adults than were left in the wilds of southern Florida at that time. Most, but not all of this collection, had come from the waters close to upper Florida Bay and had been captured by America's crocodile hunter, Argyle Hendry. Bill and Lester Piper were the Florida crocodile kings.

David Piper went along to help Lester when he responded to a crocodile complaint call from Sarasota County. A large crocodile had suddenly shown up near Osprey, a small community on Lemon Bay near Venice, and it was frightening bathers. This crocodile turned out to be nine and a half feet long and very unusually colored. It was leucistic — dark-eyed, with a white hide, but not a true pink-eyed albino. Lester made the mistake of putting it in the large crocodile pen. Within days Ironhead had killed it. The last wild-caught American crocodile to be added to the Gardens' collection was a four-footer that was caught by Don Carroll as it crossed U.S. 1 on Key Largo, in early 1956. Don brought the crocodile to Lester who kept it with the understanding Don could borrow it on occasion for the traveling menagerie that he operated as part of his duties with the Florida Game and Freshwater Fish Commission.

Photo from the author's collection.

The collection of adult American crocodiles at Everglades Wonder Gardens, in 1952. Their mouths are open for thermoregulation, a part of a crocodile's routine in warm weather.

In 1954, I began working at the Everglades Wonder Gardens full time — six days a week, nine hours a day. I was living my dream — a dream of working, in a hands-on situation, with wildlife. The female crocodiles in the Gardens' collection mated in captivity over the years but without a dry nesting site available the eggs were dropped directly in the water by the females. Occasionally Lester had managed to quickly collect a few eggs that were undamaged and remained viable. Often, some of these successfully hatched, but the overall viability was decreasing and he wanted to increase their productivity. In April, 1954, Lester put me in charge of his American crocodile propagation effort that was created out of necessity. Due to earlier passage of long overdue protection by the State of Florida and the establishment of Everglades National Park, wild crocodiles were no longer available for purchase in Florida. Lester realized that with his supply cut off, if their prized collection of crocodiles was to be maintained, then the Gardens' existing collection must produce a sufficient number of replacement animals. Then his crocodile collection would be sustained over time. He was proud of his American crocodiles, and rightly so, because at the time there was no other collection like it in the world. Many of the larger crocodiles were getting close to their maximum expected longevity, so in-house propagation was a great idea.

I would inspect the crocodile pen first thing early each morning, if Lester didn't beat me to it, throughout April into early May. If eggs were observed I'd take a long wooden pole that had on one end an attached large tin can with drain holes punched in its bottom, and drag it along the concrete bottom of the crocodile pool. I'd feel for the eggs and also listen for the telltale sound their hard shells made when the can bumped them. Using this technique, I'd then carefully scoop out any eggs the females had deposited in the water during the night. Females that were gravid[45] had no recourse but to drop them in the water because there was not any dry ground in their enclosure. Most eggs were broken because they were in the water and the crocodiles were in motion and sometimes crushed them. Some crocs tried to eat them, resulting in a high level of breakage. In 1954, I managed to collect only about a dozen fresh eggs that were not cracked. I assumed these were viable and would hatch so I buried them in a mound of sand inside an enclosure that was outside the yard. I took personal charge of the eggs and watched over them carefully until they hatched a little over two months later.

It was not exactly safe to collect the crocodile eggs. One had to stand on the wall of the pen on the narrow ledge that fronted the angled wire barrier and then lean out slightly to clear the wire with the pole. Often when dragging the pole along the bottom, great care had to be exercised to maintain your balance. If a crocodile decided to bite the pole, that sudden jerking of the pole could throw the egg dipper off balance. More than one employee came close to falling into the pen. Ralph Curtis remembers losing his balance and falling. Had the wire, which broke his fall, not caught one of his arms and a leg, it would have been disastrous. Tumbling into the crocodile pen would have been a definitive end to one's wildlife career[46]. The crocodiles were not as forgiving as the alligators.

In the seventies, Lester decided to build a connected pen and place several feet of dry sand inside it. Workers cut an access hole in the concrete wall between the two. Crocodiles could then pass between the wet and dry pens and construct nest mounds and lay eggs. This move was about twenty years too late, and although some female crocodiles took advantage of this, reproduction was never successful. By this time, most of the male and female captives were reproductively senile and incapable of producing viable sperm or eggs capable of fertilization. Over time, this once outstanding collection would dwindle as they died off. Without captive propagation occurring few American crocodiles with Florida origins would remain in the collection at Everglades Wonder Gardens. A few American crocodiles that had originated on Jamaica were purchased from wild animal dealers. Others were obtained by trading with other animal collectors and were added to the Gardens' dwindling crocodile exhibit in the 1970s.

Chapter 17

Bill Piper's Déjà Vu

BILL PIPER'S SECOND MARRIAGE was in serious trouble by 1949. His vivacious wife, Alida, had started to habitually drink to excess and was experiencing increasingly frequent bouts of deep depression and exhibiting erratic behavior. There was nothing the local medical profession could do for her and she eventually became uncontrollable. Bill feared she would harm herself. After consulting with Alida's mother, Lillian Whittle, Bill had no option other than to have his wife declared mentally incompetent and have her civilly committed into the Florida state mental hospital system. Alida became an unwilling, confined patient at the Florida State Hospital in Chattahoochee.

Bill threw himself into his work, trying to forget his personal problems. He began to inch away from operations at Everglades Wonder Gardens. In the middle of this crisis, he decided he wanted to redirect his life and embark on a course to fulfill a youthful dream. Bill Piper had always admired the lifestyle of western cowboys, and during his brief hobo career he had worked for a time on a commercial fishing boat in Alaska and as a cowhand on a working western cattle ranch. Bill made the midlife choice that he was going to be a Florida cattleman. It's unclear if Lester fully supported his older brother Bill's notion, but on January 8, 1951, the Piper brothers partnership purchased 246 acres of land in Lee County to the south of Bonita Springs and on the east side of the Tamiami Trail. This land would be the starting point for Bill's cattle ranch operation. In fact, a vacated section of the old highway was the access point to the property and this connected to the Trail on its northern end. The southern end once had reached all the way to Horse Creek, in Collier County, a distance of about two and a half miles. In March of 1953, they bought three adjoining parcels in Collier County, which totaled eighty acres. When fenced and gated the combined parcel straddled the county line with the eighty acres in Collier County and 246 acres in Lee County. They owned a long narrow pasture that in total acreage was a half-section in size.

The Piper brothers registered their cattle brand with the State of Florida. It was, "Two, Lazy Two, Pee."

$$2\sim P$$

The first few head of cattle put into the pasture were derelict or unmarketable cows that were unwanted or culled by their former owners. These were pastured temporarily, because they were destined for eventual slaughter. They would be used as food for the animals at the Wonder Gardens. Bill soon started building a permanent herd when he bought the first few head of beef cattle from Carl Williams, Sr., who had a large ranching operation between Bonita Springs and Estero. In a few years Bill and Lester would purchase several sections of land and expand their cattle ranching operation in Collier County.

On a Friday afternoon, Bill called on his friend Ray Barnes who lived with his wife in a nice piling home out on Bonita Beach. Ray was a fifty-eight-year old, Georgia-born wildlife officer, employed by the Florida Game and Fresh Water Fish Commission, and had been a resident of Bonita Springs for several years. Bill told Ray that some feral pigs were tearing up the new grass that was just sprouting in his freshly planted pasture and he wanted them removed before they tore it all up. The two men planned a hog-hunting trip for the next morning, Saturday, August 5, 1954. They would meet up at six o'clock in the morning at the cattle pens in the

Piper's Bonita Springs pasture. These wooden pens were located along the old Trail right of way in Collier County.

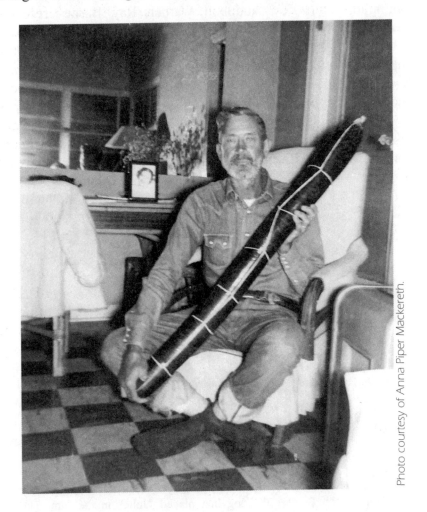

Bill Piper, at home, circa 1955. He enjoyed a brand of salami that was unavailable in Southwest Florida, so he had it shipped in. I remember being sent to the bus stop at Benson's Grocery Store to pick up full rolls of salami and other special cold cuts that had just arrived on the bus.

Ray Barnes had originally started his wildlife law enforcement career as a National Audubon Society Bird Warden, in the 1930s. He patrolled the same colonial bird rookeries in Florida Bay and the Ten Thousand Islands, and followed in the muddied footsteps of the martyred Audubon warden, Guy Bradley, who was shot and killed by the father of a plume hunter while on duty near Flamingo, in 1905. Audubon Warden Ray Barnes received recognition for his valued assistance to bird researcher, Robert P. Allen, in Allen's major dissertation, *The Roseate Spoonbill,* published in 1942, and Allen's later very popular book, *The Flame Birds*, published in 1947. Ray Barnes and Bill Piper had been buddies since the mid-forties. In 1951[47], Ray decided to accept a position as a wildlife officer with the Florida Game and Freshwater Fish Commission and continued to work out of his beachfront home near Bonita Springs.

Photo courtesy of Anna Piper Mackereth.

Bill Piper (left) with Opal, the dog that played the part of "Rip" and Ray Barnes, with Bowser the dog that played "Julie" in the film, The Yearling, 1946.

Bill was in a bad mood the morning of the planned hog hunt. He and Lester had had another of their violent arguments the night before. This time it started when Bill asked Lester if he could borrow some helpers to unload a railway carload of hundred-pound bags of grass fertilizer that he had ordered. The load was sitting on a siding waiting to be unloaded. Bill wanted some extra help from the staff at Everglades Wonder Gardens to help him unload the boxcar. Then, after it was trucked to the pasture, he would need help unloading and stacking the heavy bags in a pole shed. Bill won the argument and got promised the help he needed. To make matters worse the feral hog situation was still boiling inside of him; he'd be damned if some wild scrawny pigs were going to ruin his grass. Bill was aggravated about things in general this morning and although he had learned long ago to tolerate Lester's outbursts he wasn't going to put up with hogs or anything else damaging his pasture.

The Piper pasture had been voluntarily included in a state wildlife management area program that closed the tract to hunting. Even though he was the property owner, Bill couldn't kill the wild pigs himself because technically firearms where not permitted on land that was managed as part of such an agreement. Ray Barnes was authorized to take unprotected wildlife when it was evident the actions of animals were injurious to the property owner's primary use of the land.

When Ray arrived in his Jeep, pulling his horse trailer, Bill was waiting. His nineteen-year old nephew, David, and Bonita Springs teenager, Norman Randolph, had come in David's Jeep to help them hunt the hogs and to also search for and catch a heifer that had a known screwworm infestation and needed to be doctored. Bill had already warned the boys not to ride their horses onto the freshly planted grass because he didn't want it torn up; the hogs had already done enough damage. Ray Barnes hadn't been part of that earlier conversation. After he unloaded his horse he innocently rode over part of the sprouting grass. His horse's hoofs trampled the grass and kicked up small divots as Ray reined the horse and directed it away from the grass after Bill began yelling and cussing and generally raising hell because Ray was ruining his grass. This quickly turned into a heated argument between the two men after Ray told Bill he had a foul mouth and said, "You're not going to talk to me that way."

After several more minutes of being harangued by Bill, Ray told him, "I've had enough of your bad mouth and you can go ahead and catch your own hogs." He then told Bill he was taking his horse and his dogs and leaving. Ray Barnes walked toward the cow pen where two cow dogs; a black and white and a brindle were located. Bill intercepted Ray and yelled, "The hell you say! The brindle's my dog!" He told Ray he could take the other, the black and white animal. Ray insisted that Fort Myers veterinarian Standish Piper, who was no relation of Bill's, had given both of the dogs to him. Bill again claimed that Dr. Piper had given him the brindle dog. Ray was determined to get both dogs and started to open the gate, after Bill had warned him not to go near the gate. Bill punched Ray on the side of his face and knocked him down. Ray scrambled to his feet and at that point he glared at Bill and said, "Just hit me one more time and it'll be all over for you."

David was standing close to Ray when he heard the angry exchange of words, saw his uncle knock Ray down, and then heard Ray utter the unveiled threat to his uncle. David Piper had always heard that Ray Barnes had a short-fused temper and thought it was more than likely Ray would shoot his uncle Bill before this situation ended. David told himself, "I'm man enough to get that pistol." Instantly he responded by grabbing Ray Barnes around his arms in a bear hug and telling Bill to grab Barnes' pistol from it's holster. When Bill reached for the gun, Ray twisted, and he and David lost their balance and fell to the ground together. At that point David got in some pretty serious licks and Ray managed to bite him on the upper right arm as they continued fighting. Bill yelled, "David . . . David! Get off of him. You've already beaten him in the dirt now. You're going to hurt him." David, who was wearing spurs, dug them into Barnes' legs before he released his hold, and the two men separated. When Ray regained his feet Bill bluntly told him to get the hell out of the pasture and never come in it again unless he had his special permission. Bill held on to the .22 caliber automatic pistol, after all his brother Lester had loaned it to Ray Barnes. Ray walked away, got into his Jeep, and headed out of the pasture.

After the boys calmed down, Bill sent David and Norman to look for the heifer that needed tending to. At about the time they finished their work Ray Barnes came back to the cow pens and Bill ordered him to leave again. Bill and the boys had some canned fruit for lunch and then everyone decided it was time to head back into town. In the meantime, Ray Barnes was one furious man and had returned to his home. He first unloaded his horse and tethered the animal to a grove of nearby shade trees, and unhitched his horse trailer. He went into his house and got his twelve gauge double-barreled shotgun and a few loose shells. Next, he drove to Benson's Grocery Store in downtown Bonita Springs and bought an additional seven rounds of buckshot from clerk, Cecil Harvard. Ray Barnes headed south on the Trail, and his destination was Bill Piper's pasture.

He hadn't driven far, when Fred Wilsky from Naples waved him down. Ray Barnes pulled over and stopped. Wilsky, who had been working around Bonita Springs recently, told him that he wanted to report some illegal shooting he heard a few days ago in the game management area. Ray Barnes told him that at the moment he was in a hurry because he had to go meet a man, but said he would get in touch with him later to take the information. They parted when Ray Barnes sped off to meet the man.

David and Norman were in the lead Jeep, with Bill following a few hundred feet behind them in his, when David noticed Ray Barnes' inbound vehicle closing the gap between them. David turned his Jeep around and raced back to Bill to tell him that Barnes was back in the pasture. Bill told his nephew that he wanted him and Norman to go back, further out into the pasture, and check on the horses. He wanted them out of harm's way, well separated from him, because he had no idea why Ray Barnes was returning, and he feared that things could get out of control. The boys didn't heed his instructions and just retreated a few hundred feet down the grade and stopped. After crossing a small bridge at Snapper Creek Bill pulled his Jeep over to the side of the road.

Ray Barnes then stopped about fifty yards shy of Bill's parked Jeep and got out. Bill could see that he was carrying a weapon. At first glance it looked as though he had a high-powered rifle, but as he walked closer it became clear he was carrying a shotgun. Bill exited his Jeep and stepped to the side holding the pistol, not knowing if it was loaded of not. He cocked the automatic, pointed it in the air, and squeezed off a shot but the weapon failed to fire. He then pulled the slide and held the pistol in the air as Ray Barnes continued to advance in a crouching position while holding the shotgun in both hands and pointing the muzzle toward Bill. Bill shouted at him to stop, but Barnes didn't and continued coming toward him. Bill fired one round at him, hoping to bring him to his senses. The slug went completely through Ray's left thigh, and an instant later, while still crouched, he discharged one barrel from his hip at Bill Piper. A slug struck Bill in the left leg below the knee and he slipped, falling down on his left side onto the sloped ditch bank. He tried to get another round off but the automatic pistol had jammed. Bill was desperately trying to clear it, but in about a half-minute Ray Barnes fired the second barrel of his shotgun, and this time one slug hit Bill in the throat. Bill, still on the ground, was soon choking on his own blood and being unable to speak he raised his arm to motion David to come help him. David started forward, but Ray Barnes yelled, warning him to stay put, "No, not you. Send the other boy." Over fifty-five years later, during my interview with him, David related, "When he said that, I got my ass down in the ditch . . . I didn't want him picking me off." Norman ran to Bill and got him turned over to a point where he was able to breath a little better. David waited until Ray got into his Jeep and started to leave before he went to help his uncle.

After Ray Barnes withdrew from the field, David and Norman managed to get Bill into David's Jeep and headed for Bonita Springs to get help. The front of Bill's Jeep was riddled with buckshot and the radiator had been hit. All of the coolant had drained to the ground. David soon caught up to him and passed Ray Barnes. When he got to the pasture gate David jumped out of the Jeep, unlocked the gate, drove through the opening, and then relocked the gate to slow Ray Barnes down. David pulled in to the first place he came to with any activity where he might find some help, Tommy Reahard's Sinclair service station. Someone there grabbed a towel and this was applied to Bill's neck wound to help slow the bleeding. David told me, "Old man Downing had a Nash car and offered to take Uncle Bill on up to the hospital. I went on to the Gardens and told Daddy and he went up to the hospital."

Ray Barnes again drove to his home. After tending and wrapping his wound he telephoned Lee County Sheriff Flanders

"Snag" Thompson to report the incident. The sheriff drove down to Bonita Springs from Fort Myers and while traveling down the Trail Sheriff Thompson heard chatter on the radio. He learned that Sheriff Roy Atkins and two of his deputies were responding from the Collier County Sheriff's Department. The shooting altercation had taken place in Collier County and was out of Thompson's jurisdiction.

Both Bill Piper and Ray Barnes were treated and hospitalized at Lee Memorial Hospital in Fort Myers. When Lester arrived at the hospital his brother was undergoing emergency surgery. Bill's attending physician was Dr. Ernest Bostelman and after he had stabilized Bill he told Lester that his older brother was in very serious condition because of the neck wound's location and the fact that Bill had lost so much blood. After being satisfied that his brother was alive and receiving adequate emergency medical care Lester looked in on Ray Barnes who had been treated and admitted to the hospital. Their spoken words during their brief and intimate conversation are unknown but according to David Piper he had never seen his father so bitterly angry before he went into the room. It was not a cordial discussion . . . likely it was threatening in nature . . . should Bill Piper not make it.

Bill had a rare blood type, and the call went out for donors. Several residents of Bonita Springs, who had the matching blood type, came forward to donate blood, including Dennis Morgan's mother. Bill received three transfusions and after a long hospital stay he was released to fully recover at home. I went to visit Bill in the hospital three days after the shooting episode and he was still unable to speak and he was so heavily bandaged that he couldn't turn his head.

When released from the hospital Ray Barnes was arrested and charged with the attempted murder of Bill Piper. He was released on a $2,500.00 cash bond pending a criminal trial in Collier County. Ray lost his job with the Florida Game and Fresh Water Fish Commission because of the criminal charges and was terminated just a few months shy of his eligibility for retirement. A jury trial commenced in Everglades City, at that time the Collier County seat, on March 9, 1955, with Circuit Judge Lynn Gerald presiding. The six-man jury was sworn in at 2:10 p.m. that afternoon and the trial got started. In his opening remarks defense attorney Guy M. Strayhorn indicated that the defense would contend that Barnes shot Piper in self-defense.

Following a two-day trial, after which the jury deliberated one hour and twenty minutes, Ray Barnes was found guilty of the attempt on Bill Piper's life. He was convicted of an assault with intent to commit first-degree murder. He now faced a maximum of twenty years in prison. His attorneys immediately charged that a fair trial was impossible because of Barnes' "long service as a game warden at Bonita Springs and his rigid enforcement of the law." Defense attorney Strayhorn then filed a twenty-one-point motion for a new trial.

According to State Attorney W. Mack Smiley, the judge delayed a ruling on this motion for a new trial because the "pressure of Court business" overpowered the court reporter[48]. Judge Gerald denied the defense motion for a new trial and on June 14, 1955, he sentenced J. Ray Barnes. The judge ruled:

> "It is the judgment of the law and sentence of the court that you, Ray Barnes, for the crime for which you were and are convicted, be imprisoned in the State Penitentiary by confinement at hard labor for the term of two (2) years."

Ray Barnes' attorney immediately filed a Notice of Appeal for an appeal to the Supreme Court of Florida and a Notice for Supersedeas. Judge Gerald issued an Order of Supersedeas on June 14, 1955, and Ray Barnes was released on a $1,000.00 bond, pending the appeal. The Supreme Court finally heard the appeal during its January 1957 term. The Court ruled on March 27, 1957, to whit:

". . . And the trial judge, in declining to give the charge requested by Barnes, must have thought that Barnes' testimony as to his motives in returning to the area was, in all circumstances, so improbable as to be unworthy of belief. But however improbable, it was not demonstrably false, and the trial judge invaded the province of the jury when he disregarded it.

It was, then, error to refuse to give the charge requested by Barnes and it was clearly not harmless error. Accordingly, the judgment appealed from should be reversed and the cause remanded for a new trial."

Ray Barnes was never retried, nor incarcerated. Instead, he went to work for Latimer Maxcy (1887-1971), the wealthy owner of the Maxcy Ranch near Yeehaw Junction in Central Florida's Osceola County. Maxcy had assembled his one hundred thousand acre cattle and citrus empire in 1930[49]. Ray Barnes worked until his retirement as the Maxcy Ranch's wildlife officer. Ray Barnes was basically a good and honest man, but wasn't well liked because of his unpopular job. He got caught up in a bad situation to which he over-reacted. After retiring, Ray Barnes quietly moved back into his beachfront home on Bonita Beach and lived out his days. There is no oral or written record that indicates that Ray Barnes and Bill Piper, once close friends, ever spoke again. Ray Barnes passed away in 1973. He is interred at the Bonita Springs Cemetery with his uncle and aunt, his wife Helen who predeceased him, and two of their sons who died when small children.

Chapter 18

Scaled Danger

THERE WAS ALWAYS AN inherent risk, an element of danger, when one worked with venomous snakes, and South Florida's four species were always well represented in the Piper brothers' collection. It was necessary that the Pipers and their employees periodically make collecting trips out in the Big Cypress or the Everglades to restock the snake exhibits.

Sixteen-year old Alfred Trew often joined Bill Piper on snake collecting trips in the early years, even before the Bonita Springs Reptile Gardens was ready to open to the public. The snakes would become part of the exhibit and put on public display, in what at first were roughly made wooden aboveground enclosures that were called pits. Alfred recalled one such snake-hunting event in a 2009 interview, "I was way back out in the woods behind Naples with Luther McCormick and Bill, when I caught a water moccasin. I pinned it holding my snake hook in my right hand and caught it with my left hand. This snake was large, about four-feet long, and I had to hold it up high to clear the sack that I had opened with my right hand after I had turned loose of my hook. I got the tail in the sack and when I turned loose of the cottonmouth to drop it in the sack it turned and I got one fang right here in the thumb of my left hand . . . one fang. I didn't know if I was going to live or not. It wasn't too long and I was in misery and we still had to get out of the swamp. It was at least four hours later that they got me into the little doctor's office in Naples and it was pretty near dark by then. He looked at the bite and shook his head and said he couldn't give me any antivenin because so much time had passed since the snake had bitten me. He told them to give me plenty of water and if it started turning blue to give me strong coffee. It swelled up like a sausage . . . the side of my hand and my arm. It was a bad experience."

Alfred's hand soon became gangrenous and he nearly lost the thumb on his left hand, but because of the constant care he received at the Reptile Gardens during the aftermath of this serious snakebite; his hand began to heal. Frances Piper provided the constant nursing that Alfred needed and her concerned care included frequently soaking the hand in Epson Salts and keeping it bandaged and clean. Her care turned things around for Alfred and his hand slowly healed.

About a week after being bitten Alfred was still in excruciating pain and unable to use his hand. He couldn't work. Lester needed his help and in a not too gentle tone, with words laced with his usual profanity, Lester asked the boy, "When the hell are you going get off your ass and get back to goddamn work?" Alfred tried to explain to him just how bad his hand still hurt, but Lester wouldn't listen and ridiculed and chastised him more and told him he had better get on the ball and get back to work — and soon!

Alfred Trew recalled that it wasn't too long after this episode that Lester also received a bad bite from a big cottonmouth he had pinned and was picking up. He experienced the severe pain and major tissue damage that is so common with a cottonmouth's bite and Lester lost time from his usual nonstop pace because of the bite. Alfred said it was one of the few times that he ever knew Lester Piper to "eat crow." Lester actually apologized to Alfred for the way he had treated and spoken to him during his ordeal. In the end the cottonmouth venom had nearly destroyed the tendons in Alfred's left thumb and he would never be able to fully bend that thumb again.

Alfred was bitten again that same summer. He was on another collecting trip with Bill out on the Tamiami Trail, way out to the east of Naples. Bill was driving slow and coasted when he spotted a snake out ahead on the road in the beam of the headlights. When he stopped Bill asked Alfred to pass him a snake sack. The teenager was sound asleep in the back seat, and was not fully awake even after he heard Bill's voice rousing him. Without looking what he was doing the youngster reached up to the rear window ledge and grabbed a sack . . . then something inside the sack grabbed him. A large dusky pigmy rattlesnake, a ground rattler, had bitten him on the hand through the cloth sack. Alfred remembers this bite as being very painful and difficult to heal but it was in no way as troublesome as his first bite by the big cottonmouth.

Former Everglades Wonder Gardens guide, Ralph Curtis, remembers his first and only snakebite, and he even had an audience present to see it happen. While at work guiding a group in October 1952 Ralph Curtis tried to catch an adult pigmy rattlesnake that had managed to squeeze part way out of a narrow gap between two boards in the side of the wooden-walled snake pit in which it was housed. The snake's head was positioned at an angle and Ralph had to use his left hand to get a grip on the snake. After Ralph pinned and caught the snake around its small neck between his thumb and index finger, the still-anchored snake managed to pull it's body back and in doing so it slipped from Ralph's grip and bit his index finger with one fang.

Ralph excused himself and took the snake over to another pit and dropped it inside — where a large indigo snake instantly grabbed the little rattlesnake and ate it. Ralph went into the butcher room and told Don Carroll what had happened. Don immediately proceeded to perform snakebite first aid — the standard cut and suck technology of the day. The fang puncture was opened, enlarged with a sharp pocketknife, and then a suction bulb from a snakebite kit was applied in an effort to remove as much of the venom from the puncture as possible. Lester then told Ralph to go home and soak his hand in Epson Salts, mixed in the hottest water he could stand to put his hand into. He did that for the rest of the day, but by bedtime his hand was throbbing and felt like it was on fire. Ralph could get about thirty seconds of temporary relief by swinging the hand over his head. He had a nearly sleepless night.

By morning Ralph's hand was black and swollen up to his wrist and there was general tenderness in his armpit. Ralph told Lester that he thought he should see a doctor but it was Lester's opinion that he should just keep soaking his hand in Epson Salts. Later, as the color of Ralph's hand darkened, Lester conceded. He told Ralph to go to Naples and see Dr. James Craig who was familiar with the treatment of snakebites.

The doctor looked at the bite and gave Ralph something to help alleviate the pain and told him the venom had already caused the development of gangrene in his finger. Dr. Craig told Ralph, "I can either cut your finger off right now, or we can try something new that I've read about that was used for treating gangrenous frostbite in the Korean War." Ralph opted for the new treatment, rather than having his finger amputated. This consisted of putting Ralph's hand in an elevated splint that would hold his hand up above his head. Then his entire arm, from his armpit to the affected hand, was wrapped in elastic bandage and he was sent home. He would return on a schedule and each time the doctor would remove dead skin and redress the wound. Finally, after one of the painful trimmings, Jim Craig announced, "I can see new pink skin and that tells me that blood is getting to your finger." He then told Ralph he didn't think he would lose his digit, but it would remain somewhat disfigured.

Monday, October 15, 1956, started out as just another regular workday. I had finished most of my pre-opening chores and everything seemed normal except I happened to notice that Lester was standing alone at the rattlesnake pit. He had both hands on the railing and with his head bowed he seemed to be staring down at the snakes through the angled glass. He appeared to be in deep thought when I picked up the dry rags and started wiping the heavy dew from the pit railings so customers wouldn't get their clothing wet. As I wiped I slowly made my way toward him. When I got close enough I spoke to him for the first time, "Good morning, Lester." He hesitantly raised his head and looked at me and I could see that he was crying and his face was tear-streaked. He wiped his eyes and rubbed his face dry with a handkerchief, looked at me and said, "It's not a very good morning at all, Charlie . . . Don Carroll died yesterday." "What! . . . what did you just say?" I stuttered in shock and disbelief. All choked up, Lester continued, "Don was bitten by a goddammed rattlesnake on Saturday and he died yesterday. Jackye called last night and told me. He's dead." Lester's words sunk in and I began to cry with him. We just stood there next to each other sobbing and then an awesome almost reverent silence followed the tears. This lasted for a few moments more. After we had composed ourselves Lester finally ambled away and went inside his kitchen. I should have gone home right then and there, because I wasn't worth a damn for the rest of the day and wouldn't be for several days thereafter. When we first met over four years earlier my father posed the question, "Aren't you afraid of being bitten by a poisonous snake, Don?" He had replied, "Oh, hell no. I will be some day . . . but it won't kill me." His words were still ringing through my head.

Over time, if any employee at Everglades Wonder Gardens was ever truly allowed to get it ajar and successfully open the heavy-duty gate to get inside Lester Piper's self-created wall, it was Don Carroll. During the relatively short time that Don worked for Lester the two men grew extremely close. At the time of his death, Don's second child, a daughter, was only nine months old and she had been named after Lester Piper. Her name is Leslye.

Twenty-eight year old Don Carroll was working in Perry, Florida, on October 13, when his tragic accident occurred. After he left the Wonder Gardens he took a job as an Education Officer with the Florida Game and Freshwater Fish Commission. He spent much of his time on the road driving a tractor-trailer rig. The trailer was partitioned off into cages, which contained live specimens of Florida wildlife. Don would roam through Florida and set up his traveling menagerie for scheduled exhibits at schools, fairs, and other public events. He had arrived in Perry to lecture on snakes and other Florida wildlife at the annual Taylor County Pine Tree Festival. During his presentation on Florida's snakes, Don had a live five-foot eastern diamondback rattlesnake out on the elevated stage. He held a long stick that had a balloon tethered to it and he was trying to get the snake to strike the balloon to demonstrate the rattlesnake's speed. As he talked, the excited snake ignored the balloon and tried to crawl off the platform and into the audience.

Photo courtesy of Warren Boutchia.

An admirable personality, a man of character, and everyone's friend, Don Carroll, at Everglades Wonder Gardens, in 1953.

Don continued to reach out and bring the snake back to center stage by pulling it back toward his person with his snake hook, but this rattlesnake was fresh-caught, nervous, and determined to get away. Fearing for the safety of the people, Don tried to stop the rattler from moving ahead by stepping on it. With that ill-fated move, the snake displayed very unusual behavior — an element that Don wasn't expecting. It suddenly thrashed and threw the front part of its body around to Don's rear. Fully extended, it struck and both of its fangs penetrated the back of Don's unprotected left leg just above his snake-proof boot, on which he had relied for his personal safety. Apparently, the venom was injected directly into an artery and ultimately there was little hope for Don's survival. Despite valiant medical efforts to save his life, including administration of voluminous antivenin, blood transfusions, and use of an "iron lung", Don died in a Tallahassee hospital twenty-two hours later.

Don Carroll had apparently neglected to "milk" the rattlesnake before working with it in public. This is a procedure that most poisonous snake handlers go through to reduce the amount of the snake's injectible venom should they be accidentally bitten or struck — there is a difference. When it is to be milked a "hot" fully loaded snake is pinned and picked up with a good grip behind the snake's head. Then the handler forces the snake to bite through a tight membrane covering a container, most often a glass receptacle. The venom glands, which are located on either side of the snake's head behind the eyes, are then pressed and massaged to squeeze out as much venom as possible from the snake's venom glands via the hollow, hypodermic needle-like fangs. Years later, some Sunday morning snake catchers would be critical after learning that a few surviving eyewitnesses claimed that Don failed to take this step before he started his ill-fated program.

Employees of the Gardens weren't the only ones who were exposed and received venomous snakebites around Bonita Springs. Other people who didn't work for the Pipers but who were in need of cash often managed to catch coral snakes, cottonmouths, and both species of rattlesnakes they encountered. These were usually scooped into a box or a trash barrel and brought to the Gardens. Some people would take the risk and try to catch a specimen alive by hand for that guaranteed five dollar bill — the price Lester usually paid for an average sized adult eastern diamondback rattlesnake. After October 15, 1956, whenever Lester told one of us at the Gardens to respond to a telephone call about a rattlesnake being in someone's yard somewhere close to Bonita Springs, we took along a snake hook and a large fine-meshed cloth hoop net that had a very deep bag. Lester Piper was very insistent that none of us would pin and pick up a rattlesnake and drop it in a snake sack anymore. Following Don Carroll's untimely death, the ground rules changed and venomous snake handling became much safer at Everglades Wonder Gardens. The specimen would be brought back to the Gardens in the tightly twisted shut net, taken to the rattlesnake pit and released into it without ever being touched by anyone. If it were an extra large, fine specimen it would be placed in a freestanding glass-fronted cage along the sidewalk in the yard.

Luther McCormick's son David (1935-1983), had spent most of the night at O'Conner's Bamboo Tavern[50] in downtown Bonita Springs trying to drink the place dry. After partaking in the last call at closing he had managed to make it to the family home two and a half miles south of Bonita Springs in Collier County. The house the McCormicks lived in at the time was located on the west side of the Trail. It was accessible by driving one hundred yards or so up the abandoned railroad grade of the Seaboard Air Line Railroad. The tracks and ties had been removed years before when the rail line found the Naples destination to be unprofitable and merged with its rival, the Atlantic Coast Line Railroad, to form the Seaboard Coast Line Railroad.

David had made it safely home and was in bed sleeping it off. He had only been asleep for about four hours when his mother suddenly awakened him. She was upset and told him that there was a big rattlesnake out in the yard near her clothesline. She asked her son to get out of bed right away and go outside and kill the snake. David dressed and staggered outside, still half asleep, to find the diamondback. He was not an experienced catcher of poisonous snakes, but in his mind's eye he saw at least a crisp five-dollar bill — or maybe he envisioned a dozen or more cold beers — on the ground in front of him. The snake's tightly coiled body was positioned in the species' defensive lateral "S" position. The big snake's tongue periodically flickered out in David's direction as the snake tried to determine what this threat was that it was facing. All the while the loose, dry, dead skin segments of its pulsating rattle sang loudly in the otherwise still morning. On unsteady legs and with an unclear head, David McCormick reached for something to pin the snake's head to the ground. After a few attempts he had it pressed down tight against the sand. He was ready, and as he tried to focus his eyes, he reached down to clamp his right hand around the rattler's head as he had watched his father and the Piper brothers do so many times. His grip was apparently inappropriate, perhaps too far behind the snake's head, because the rattler was able to turn it's head around some distance and managed to sink its two long fangs into the flesh of David's right hand, between his thumb and his forefinger.

David was transported to the brand new Naples Community Hospital and treated by the staff's snakebite specialist, Dr. William Bailey. Dr. Bailey administered quantities of polyvalent antivenin

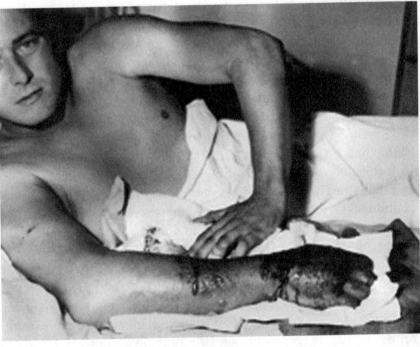

Photo courtesy of Bob Garrison.
Used by permission of the McCormick family.

David McCormick, circa twenty-four-hours after he was bitten in the right hand by a large eastern diamondback rattlesnake. The swelling would eventually reach his shoulder. This was a serious snakebite, and it had a bad ending.

to counteract the haemotoxic rattlesnake venom. When black and blue swelling began to envelop David's right hand and started to spread up his arm, Dr. Bailey called for ice and packed David's hand and arm completely in it up to his shoulder, trying to slow the spread of necrosis and minimize the venom's affect. As the swelling increased, and the darkening skin began to balloon, individual incisions were made in David's grotesquely swollen hand and limb in an attempt to relieve pressure and drain more of the deadly venom from his system. The hand and arm had changed in color from blue to black and even though he was sedated the level of nearly unbearable pain mounted. Dr. Bill Bailey was a former military surgeon who was highly skilled. He worked through the night and he managed, almost miraculously, to save David McCormick's life — and his limb and hand. Well, at least for a while.

David was released from the hospital and instructed to return on a date specific to have Dr. Bailey check out his hand and have the dressing changed. He failed to do so. David did return to O'Conner's and the story goes that after a few rounds of beer one of his drinking buddies wanted to see the bite. David slowly unwrapped the bandage to expose the site and his pinkie and ring finger came off with the bandage. The hand was severely gangrenous and the two digits had literally rotted off.

David made another trip to the Naples Hospital and Dr. Bailey had no choice but to amputate his right hand at the wrist. Unfortunately, David McCormick's snakebite experience didn't end there, because the amputation that had been made at the joint continued to drain. David was sent to consult specialists and surgeons at Jackson Memorial Hospital in Miami, who had no other option but to remove David's forearm halfway between the wrist and the elbow.

Even after his retirement Bill Piper continued to catch rattlesnakes that he found. Most eastern diamondback rattlesnakes refuse to eat in captivity, so Bill only kept those that would willingly accept food. Those that wouldn't eat readily were taken out to some wild place and released. In 1979 he was keeping four of them captive in cages at his home. Bill was offering a particular snake a dead rat and was holding the rat by its tail while dangling the animal through a small feeding door in the top of the cage. He was teasing the snake, trying to attract it to the still-warm food item. Finally, he had the snake's full attention and the rattler struck at the rat at about the same time Bill gave it another shake and simultaneously moved it aside slightly. The rattlesnake missed the rat but caught one of Bill's fingers. This snakebite event was kept mostly quiet but Bill had received a really bad life-threatening bite. Before it was over the elderly man nearly lost his arm but he refused to get rid of the snakes — unless, he told his wife, she could find them a good home.

My telephone rang one Saturday, and it was Bill Piper's wife, Emie. I hadn't seen or talked to her in a few years, although she and my wife were once very close friends. In fact the last time I talked to Emie was a couple of years before when Jean and I ran into her and Bill at a Conway Twitty and Loretta Lynn concert at the Lee County Civic Center. After pleasantries, Emie said, "Charles, I've got to get rid of these damn rattlesnakes that Bill has here at the house." I didn't know that Bill Piper was still keeping live diamondbacks. She continued, "He's going to get himself killed fooling with them like he does. I told him I was going to call you to see if you'd take them. He said you could have them." I thought this offer over for a few minutes although I knew from the beginning that I had to decline the invitation to take the collection of captive rattlesnakes. I had no place to keep them. I offered to take them with the understanding that I would set them free somewhere on a large tract of public-owned land where they would be safe. When I suggested that, Emie replied, "No, he don't want them turned loose. He says some damn fool would just kill them, and he doesn't want to take them to the Gardens." I wanted to help but under the conditions I had to decline taking the snakes. More time passed and finally Bill's son Wiley Piper (1963-2006) was told to take the rattlesnakes to Everglades Wonder Gardens and he did. Had the choice of where they should go been Wiley's, his sister Anna is sure he would have preferred to release them.

Chapter 19

Bear Hunting With Bill Piper

IN LATE APRIL, 1958, a half-grown Florida black bear wandered into Naples from out of the woods to the east of the city and someone saw it when it ducked into a wooded city block fairly close to Crayton Cove on Naples Bay. Everglades Wonder Gardens was notified immediately, and while Bill and David Piper started to gather and load equipment and horses onto trailers, Lester asked Wildlife Biologist Bob Garrison of the Florida Game and Freshwater Fish Commission if I could ride along with him to Naples. Bob was already responding to the bear call and was getting ready to leave for Naples in his Jeep. Bob and I were to try and find the bear's specific location, and after Bill and David arrived we'd group together and try to catch the bear alive. That was the general plan.

Naples' new radio station, WNOG, aired the bear's presence in town as a news bulletin and before we knew it everybody in Naples had converged on the scene. An important aspect of this event was that my wife Jean's and my friends, Jimmie and Sue Jones, lived next to us in another apartment. They had left Naples a few weeks prior for Brunswick, Georgia, when Jimmie went on active duty with the U.S. Navy.

By the time Bill arrived, the bear was still hiding in the densely wooded group of vacant lots near Crayton Cove, so he formulated a new plan. He told me, "Charlie, I want you to take some ropes and go over to the marina and ask them if you can borrow a skiff. We can use it to catch this bear. Get a few volunteer helpers out of this crowd to row it out in the bay for you, and you wait on dead ready. Me and Dave will use the horses and with the dog's help we'll run the bear east into the water and get it swimming and then you'll be able to get a rope around it and hold onto it until we can bring up our cage and take it off your hands."

Before he rode off Bill never told me what I was supposed to do when I had a rope around the bear's neck and it decided it wanted to climb in the boat with us. I managed to borrow a boat and found a couple of volunteers brave enough to help. While I was rigging a lariat they rowed me far enough offshore that we would have a clear shot once the bear got into the water. Bill's plan started to work, at first, until the bear broke out of the woods and reached the centerline of Tenth Street. When they saw the bear the crowd on both sides of its route made a simultaneous roar. Then the mass of curious people began to surge toward the animal. The frightened bruin stopped, turned around, and started to run back west. It loped past the posse and evaded the dogs that had earlier been on its heels. Bill and David turned their horses and followed. Once it broke out of the woods into a residential area, the bear never slowed. It made a course adjustment making a ninety-degree turn northward and continued running at full speed. It may seem incredulous, but the new route brought it smack dab into our apartment building where it narrowly missed our bedroom window by only a few feet and crashed through the former bedroom window of Jimmie and Sue Jones. Thankfully, new tenants hadn't moved in yet. Inside the apartment the bear exited the bedroom and moved to the opposite outside wall. It first went to the kitchen door where it stood on its rear legs and raked its fore claws down the screen but the jalousie glass sections didn't give way. It moved a few feet to the right, jumped up on the cabinet top and broke through the glass, leaping out the kitchen window. The bear raced on northward until it reached First Avenue, South, near the First United Methodist Church of Naples. It quickly scaled a stout and tall pine tree where it rested and trembled in fear and exhaustion. The citizenry of Naples heard about the bear's new location over the airwaves, and soon scores of people surrounded the tree. In the meantime, those of us from the Wonder Gardens brought up our equipment and gathered at the base of the tree ready to try and make a live capture. My old classmate at Naples High School, Edward Jones, who was a gung-ho city policeman, was on scene along with a few others from the department. Ed announced to his cohorts, "If that bear comes down that tree, shoot it." Our capture crew looked at each in disbelief. Here we were, all set up ready to try and make a live capture of a two hundred-fifty-pound bear and a cop on an ego trip spews something like that out of his mouth! This was in the days before animal tranquilizer darts were in use and we were going to try and use nets and then drag the tangled bear inside a secure box.

Unfortunately, the bear decided to come down the tree before Bill Piper could resolve Ed's "shoot to kill" utterance with the police officers on scene. Better crowd control by the trigger-happy police department would have been more helpful. When the bear had slid about halfway down the pine, Officer Fred Scott drew and fired all the bullets from his six-shot .38 caliber revolver into the animal, but the bear kept coming down the tree. When it reached the ground the poor creature tried to drag itself away. A Naples resident, a private citizen, ran to his truck and grabbed a high-powered rifle. With one well-placed shot he put the dying bear out of its misery.

Chapter 20

Tragedy Strikes Again

LESTER PIPER'S OLDEST GRANDDAUGHTER, among a total of five grandchildren, was Anthia Jill Piper. In 1976, she and her parents lived in a comfortable home near the Everglades Wonder Gardens on South Riverside Drive that was once among the series of lots owned by Bill and Lester. Sixteen-year-old Jill had met an older man, a twenty-four-year old by the name of Harold Eugene Lucas, who was a resident of Bonita Springs. He had been born in Arkansas and was known among his peers as one who abused both alcohol and drugs. The couple started dating and at Jill's behest Lester gave Gene Lucas a job at the Wonder Gardens.

The couple's relationship was to be short-lived and by the early part of August the constant quarrels between them began to intensify into more serious arguments. David and Eleanor Piper were concerned and issued warnings to Lucas, demanding that he stay away from their daughter and their residence. Gene Lucas was apparently mentally unstable, or habitually under the influence of some bad drugs, because their words did not deter him. He returned to the Piper home and the Lee County Sheriff's Department ended up arresting him for trespassing on August tenth. He posted a cash bond and was released from the Lee County Jail on the same day.

On Friday night, August 13, 1976[51], the Piper family had gone on a planned weekend camping trip, but Jill wanted to remain at home. She connected up with some friends and during the early evening they encountered Gene Lucas a few times around town. He appeared to be somewhat intoxicated and made some serious threats against Jill's safety and welfare; threatening her with bodily harm. Jill and two friends, seventeen-year old Terri Rice and nineteen-year old Richard Byrd, returned to the Piper residence and Jill immediately armed herself with a shotgun and a .38 pistol from among her father's firearms. Initially, they had parked a car across the street, but after midnight they decided to move it into the driveway in the event they had to leave quickly should Lucas show up to make good on his threats. When they went across the street to move the car Jill still held the shotgun, and Richard was inside the home and armed with the pistol. The girls drove the car into the driveway, exited the car, and started walking toward the house when they saw Lucas standing next to the building. He raised and aimed a .22 rifle and fired at Jill. She fell to her knees on the lawn and Terri ran inside the front door to tell Richard that Jill had been shot. Terri then continued into the bedroom and telephoned the Sheriff's Department. Richard joined Terri near the master bedroom just before Lucas broke through the front door brandishing a shotgun, the one Jill had in her possession earlier, and the rifle. Terri and Richard were crouched, cowering in the hallway off the master bedroom. When Richard stood up he saw the barrel of the shotgun first, then Lucas came around the corner into the hall. He was cradling the .22 caliber rifle in his arms. He raised the shotgun and shot Richard in the stomach, knocking him down. Terri ran into the bathroom and tried to hold the door closed but Lucas managed to push his way in. Terri struggled, trying to hold herself against him so he couldn't raise the gun to shoot her. She continued to talk to him, telling him the Sheriff's Department was on their way, and not to shoot anyone else. He told her he would leave, so she released him. He started out of the bathroom and spun around as Terri slammed the door shut. He tried to push it open again a couple of times then fired through the closed door. Pellets struck Terri in the abdomen. Lucas turned and looked at Richard then pushed him with his foot as he held the muzzle of the shotgun about ten inches from his face, but the shotgun did not fire. Gene Lucas then left the house.

Gene Lucas shot Jill Piper a total of five times with the rifle, hitting her three times in the back and twice in the head. She fell unconscious on the lawn of her parent's home and according to the medical examiner she was dead within seconds. By the time authorities arrived on the scene Gene Lucas had run into the night and disappeared.

Every one of us who knew the Piper family was crushed because of their loss. Locals in Bonita Springs feared for their safety knowing a madman murderer was on the loose in their community. An intense manhunt was launched for the killer that involved multi-agency participation from Lee and Collier counties, but day after day, horse-mounted posses, even bloodhounds, came up empty-handed and helicopter flyovers failed to find a trace of Lucas. Four days after the murder and shootings, southwest Florida was rife with rumors. The most repeated one was — law enforcement agencies were unable to locate and capture the fugitive, and they never would, because the Piper's had already found him and he was slowly being digested in the stomachs of several large crocodiles that had torn him apart. The most elaborate rendition of this story was that Bill and Lester Piper had even thrown him in the crocodile pen while he was still alive. The more time that passed without him being physically apprehended the more reasonable these rumors sounded.

Seven days after Jill Piper's cold-blooded murder Lucas came out of the woods and walked into the MacDonald's Restaurant in North Naples and ordered a hamburger. A customer recognized him and the Collier County Sheriff's Department was notified. Two deputies arrived on the scene, but by the time they got there Lucas had left the restaurant and was last seen headed back into the woods. The deputies commandeered a customer's Jeep and ran the fugitive down in a clump of palmettos. After the second time a deputy shouted the order for him to come out of hiding and surrender, he did, and was promptly arrested. Gene Lucas was transported to the Lee County Jail and charged with first-degree murder in the death of Jill Piper, and the attempted first-degree murder of Terri Rice and Richard Byrd.

After his granddaughter's death, Lester seemed to withdraw into himself. He would sit in one of his favorite chairs and just shake his head. Lester just couldn't comprehend why she had been snuffed out so early. Bill Piper couldn't believe that such a thing had happened and tried to understand why this idiot had to take Jill's life. He questioned how long the couple had known one another, and been together. He was stunned when he learned they had been dating for not much more than a month. Bill was forlorn about the whole affair and it seemed odd to him that the killer could have taken his grand niece's life so easily.

Ken Morrison was living and working at Everglades Wonder Gardens during this very difficult time for the Piper family. Ken shared some of Lester's reactions with me, "When his granddaughter got killed . . . got murdered, Lester was worried about me being in the cottage that was behind the butcher house. That's where I stayed. He came out there one night — I was still working and it was nine o'clock at night . . . I had the light on and I was cutting stuff up. Lester said, 'I hate to know you're not armed out here. This crazy bastard will come in here and shoot you through the window!' I said, 'Well you ought to worry about that when I walk around here at midnight when you're sitting in the kitchen reading the newspaper, with the light on.' Anyway he passed me this .38 pistol, and said, 'Here take this, I had to take it off a deputy up in Wyandotte.' I said, 'What?' Lester replied, 'I'll tell you that story some other time.' I managed to get the story out of him one evening a little later on. The law had been chasing them by boat and they ran the boat Lester was in into shallows and they ended up aground. Lester had to jump overboard to escape and he ran for the woods. The officers went into the woods after him. 'I saw him and inched up to him. He was shaking so much I just walked up and took this gun off of him.' I interrupted him, and said, 'You just walked up to a guy with a loaded gun?' He answered, 'You could tell he wasn't going to shoot anybody.' That was the wildest thing I ever heard about either one of them doing."

Ken also recalled that a day or two after Jill's murder two young men walked into the Gardens and told Ken that they wanted to talk to Lester Piper. "I told them I'd see if he was free to talk and I went inside the butcher room and told Lester they were here and asked him if he wanted to talk to them. He looked outside to check them out and asked me, 'Do you know who they are?' I didn't know anyone around Bonita Springs except people at the Wonder Gardens, and I told him I didn't recognize them. They weren't dressed very well, one of them had on tennis shoes and cut-off jeans. Lester said, 'You come out there with us,' and he reached into the drawer where he kept the pistol that he he used to shoot horses with. He tucked that down in his pocket. We walked outside and walked up to the two men. The one who had spoken to me earlier, said, 'You're Lester Piper?' Lester acknowledged that he was, and at the same time he was carefully sizing them both up. The guy then said, 'I need to talk to you alone.' Lester didn't flinch as he turned and looked him straight in the eyes again, and told him, 'Whatever you've got to say you can say in front of this man right here, if you want to say something.' Then their purpose for the visit came out, when the guy said, 'Mr. Piper, I don't know you, but for ten thousand dollars I'll lay this guy (Lucas) on your doorstep for you. I'll bring him to you.' Lester looked down for a second, and then looking the guy straight in his eyes he squinted when he said, 'You guys get off my goddammed property.' They left.

That happened on a Saturday night and on the following Monday afternoon I was outside the gate and saw a gray Lincoln Continental come by, and then it turned around and pulled in and parked near the gate. I watched as the driver got out of the car and stepped back to the rear door and opened it. Then this old frail-looking man swung his legs around to face me. He introduced himself, but his name escapes me. Then he said, 'I'm looking for Mr. Piper.' It turned out that this was someone who Lester once did work for in Michigan. He had heard about Jill's murder on the news and he came to see if Lester needed any help. I went inside to get Lester and told him who was outside in the parking lot and wanted to see him. He walked out to the guy sitting in the car and his face lit up like it does when someone recognizes somebody they like and haven't seen for a while. The man said to Lester, 'I heard about your problems and I came by to let you know that whatever I have you can use . . . 'Lester interrupted him, and said, 'Nope, there's nothing anybody can do, she's already dead. I guess they'll catch this guy.' He turned to me, and said, 'It's okay, and you can go back inside now.'" The two old partners in whiskey crime had a brief reunion.

On January 14, 1977, Harold Eugene Lucas was found guilty, as charged, of one count for the premeditated first-degree murder of Anthia Jill Piper by shooting her with a firearm. Additionally he was convicted on two other counts. These were for the attempted premeditated murders of Terri Rice by shooting her with a firearm and Richard Byrd by shooting him with a firearm. Following the recommendation of the jury, Gene Lucas was sentenced to death for Jill Piper's murder. He was also sentenced to thirty years each for the other two charges. At the time of this writing several appeals by Lucas have failed and he has been on Florida's death row for over three decades. Among those condemned persons, Gene Lucas has one of the longest tenures on Florida's death row.

There was another tragedy at Everglades Wonder Gardens and it occurred much earlier. Warren Boutchia was there and remembers it this way; "The saddest thing that ever happened during my time at the Everglades Wonder Gardens happened in 1954[52]. Fifteen-year old Gordon Bullard was a Bonita Springs teenager who worked at the Gardens part-time, after school and on weekends. He and I were loading fill dirt into a wheelbarrow from a pile behind the panther cages at the back of the yard. We then took turns and pushed the load along the ditch bank on the outside of the fence to the rip rapped slope along the river. We were filling little places where dirt had washed-out after a heavy rain. Gordon was a hard worker and we were talking as we shoveled dirt into the wheelbarrow. Suddenly, and without saying anything, Gordon dropped to the ground. I thought he had just fainted and I tried to revive him but I couldn't. Charlie LeBuff was guiding near the deep turtle pen, I could hear him talking, so I dashed through the gate and told him what had happened. He spoke to the people in his tour, and asked, 'Is there a doctor in this group?' There was, and

I led the doctor to Gordon. The doctor tried, and tried, but could not resuscitate him. Gordon Bullard was dead! Everyone at the Gardens was affected, as was the entire Bonita Springs community, because of the loss of Gordon at such a young age. He was a popular kid and well-liked, so we all moped around for quite a while after that."

Chapter 21

Snake Hunting With Lester Piper

FROM THE BEGINNING, THE Everglades Reptile Gardens' wildlife collection contained a variety of species and multitudes of specimens of native south Florida snakes. As the attraction evolved over time, snakes were a major part of the advertised "2,000 specimen" collection. In the early days Bill and Lester had the time and enjoyed going out in the field and catching snakes themselves.

They knew all of the primary habitats where, at any time, a particular species could be found and captured. They always preferred big individuals of the larger showy species because size was important for their exhibits and the sight of big snakes helped to satisfy their customers. As time passed, the brothers began to rely on area residents to bring in specimens as their responsibilities grew. When large mammals and birds became part of their growing menagerie they demanded more time-consuming specialized care than crocodilians, turtles, and snakes.

Periodically, the snake collection dwindled, because many specimens were periodically released if they failed to accept food in captivity. When conditions were right, Lester would take an employee or two along on an excursion to collect more snakes. Before I became an employee of Everglades Wonder Gardens I had first snake-hunted with Ralph Curtis a few times in 1953 around Bonita Springs before venturing afield on my own to look for more of the interesting species I wanted to see and capture. Some of the exceptional snakes I caught, like big, yellow rat snakes and eastern diamondback rattlesnakes were taken to Lester, and he paid me for them. After I became one of his employees, he no longer offered to purchase specimens from me. He expected me to contribute those I didn't want to his collection or release them. I was invited and had the great experience of accompanying Lester on two collecting trips before he ended his active collecting. Growing demands on his time at the Gardens precluded nights in the field, and he missed that element of the wildlife business, as he grew older.

My first collecting trip with Lester Piper involved a long road trip by Jeep that took us out to the east into the Everglades and beyond Forty-Mile Bend on the Tamiami Trail. It would be an all-nighter and the sun, still obscured by storm clouds, would be rising by the time we returned to Bonita Springs the next morning. Thank goodness I was off work on the day after, but Lester did his full routine without getting any sleep. It was early September and it was pouring rain. A tropical depression was moving across the southern Florida peninsula, and when Lester had heard the weather reports a few days before the system was supposed to reach the state and affect our weather, he organized this collecting trip. Heavy rains when the wetlands were already flooded optimized the opportunities for collecting, increasing the availability of snakes exposed on the highway.

Lester, Warren Boutchia, and I left the Gardens about an hour before dark because Lester told us he wanted to be on the other side of Naples at about the time night fell. The plan was that once we got to the eastern outskirts of Naples we would reduce speed and drive slowly, about ten to fifteen miles per hour through the torrential rain, looking for snakes that were leaving the flooded wetlands to reach the higher ground that the highway shoulder and pavement provided. I had never done any serious road collecting before so it was a whole new experience for my nineteen years. Traffic was extremely light because few sane motorists wanted to make the Everglades crossing at night to reach Miami during inclement weather. Speeding automobiles negotiating the curved Trail often hydroplaned during these weather conditions and many cars, their drivers, and passengers had been lost in the deep canal that bordered the Tamiami Trail[53]. This was a rare night that was created especially for snake hunters. Each of us wore battery-powered headlamps, each had a snake hook with which to pin poisonous snakes or savage but harmless species, and the Jeep was well stocked with empty feed sacks in which we would bag our specimens. Lester drove on through the pelting rain as the headlights reached out, striking countless drops of wind-driven rain that raced in sheets across the pavement driven by strong wind gusts. The vacuum-operated windshield wipers were slow and visibility was poor as we plowed through the blinding rain. The leaking canvas top of the Jeep billowed and slapped in the wind repeatedly with every gust. If the wind increased much more we would be afield during a tropical storm.

We had stopped and picked up a few specimens after leaving Naples and had reached a point a few miles west of Royal Palm Hammock[54] when I yelled, "Snake!" Lester slowed to a stop.

There, illuminated in the Jeep's headlights on the blacktop a few yards in front of us was a huge Florida kingsnake. I recognized it from the distance as to species and since I excitedly exclaimed I had never caught a kingsnake before, I was invited to step outside into the pelting rain and catch it. I was drenched by the time I walked the few feet and when I reached down with my hand and picked the snake up about mid-body it responded by quickly coiling around my arm. Then the kingsnake turned its head and pressed it against my skin and slid it's closed mouth down the side of my wrist. It must have found a spot it liked and opened its mouth wide, bit me, and began to actively chew. Multitudes of sharp recurved teeth were making mincemeat out of my skin, and it really hurt. Knowing that Lester and Warren were watching me, I accepted that I would have to just grin and bear it. My rainwater-mixed blood was soon dripping from my arm. Not wanting to harm the non-poisonous specimen by just jerking it loose and leaving teeth imbedded in my skin, I waited for it to quit gnawing and turn me loose before I dropped it into the open sack I had pulled loose from my belt and shook open with my free hand.

Before we had reached Forty-Mile Bend we had selectively captured dozens of snakes. These included venomous cotton-mouths and pigmy rattlesnakes, Florida water snakes, Florida green water snakes, eastern mud snakes[55], striped crayfish snakes[56], peninsular ribbon snakes, and more kingsnakes. Incidental to snakes we also had jointly collected a bagful of pig and leopard frogs that were caught in the act of hopping across the road. These would be later used for water snake food, but from the conversation inside the Jeep it was clear that some of the legs of the larger pig frogs were going to be cooked in a pan on the electric hotplate back in the slaughterhouse at the Gardens.

At the junction of what today is known as Krome Avenue and U.S. 27 we turned around and headed back for Bonita Springs at a slightly increased speed, still selecting and picking up a few other large snakes from the road. In 1954, the small bridges along the Trail were wooden. Periodically Lester would stop at a bridge and we would all get out in the warm rain and hunt under the bridges. Here we found enormous yellow rat snakes that were coiled in the timber framework of the bridge. This unique rat snake habitat would disappear in the near future when the state road department started to replace the original wooden structures with concrete box culverts[57]. The snake hunt proved to be very successful and we made it back, all of us bloody and wet and cold, to Bonita Springs as the eastern horizon was brightening through the still-pouring rain.

Ralph Curtis made one memorable night snake-collecting trip with Lester and Don Carroll, in 1953. They drove down the Trail then turned north on State Road 29. North of Immokalee they connected to State Road 82, which reached Fort Myers and connected back with the Trail to reach Bonita Springs. Ralph remembers catching a variety of snakes on this trip, but the most vivid recollection is the number of very large Florida green water snakes they encountered at a flooded site along State Road 82.

My second collecting trip with Lester proved to be radically different than the first. It was a dry season collecting trip, in early May 1955, before the summer rainy season began. This time it was Lester, his son David, and me. That I was going to be in the field with Lester and his son — just the three of us — was awesome and has remained one of my most memorable experiences. We left the

Gardens in David's Jeep before dark. I was told we were headed for a certain, but apparently unnamed, cypress head in the Piper's Bonita Springs pasture.

Bill Piper with a huge cottonmouth from a cypress head in the Piper's Bonita Springs pasture.

Photo courtesy of Anna Piper Mackereth.

Once inside the pasture we stopped along the side of the road at the spot where Bill and Lester usually placed the skulls of dead animals to deteriorate as part of the process of defleshing them. Two enormous skulls were in the process of being cleaned; one was that of an alligator and the other a crocodile. Both animals had died from natural causes in recent months and their carcasses were beheaded. The body parts had been deposited elsewhere in another section of the pasture. The skulls were treated differently. They were each completely wrapped in burlap and then covered with strong wire and staked to the ground so carrion-eating birds and animals couldn't drag them off or disarticulate the bone. In short order ants and dermastid beetles would find them and remove every trace of tissue from the bone. In the end, the skulls would be complete, each tooth would be in place, and they would be housed in the Gardens museum or traded with private collectors or museums for other skulls that were missing from the Piper's collection.

One of these collectors was Jim Kenefick from Danielson, Connecticut. Jim, his wife, and two sons would visit Bonita Springs each winter for a couple of weeks and exchange animal skulls from their large private collection with Lester and Bill. Another skull collector was Gordon Hubbell, D.V.M. Doctor Hubbell was the director of the Crandon Park Zoo[58] then located on Key Biscayne, near Miami. Dr. Hubbell remembers the Piper brothers, "I actually knew Bill better than Lester because I used to trade skulls of zoo animals to Bill for alligator heads. In the early half of the twentieth century, small "roadside zoos" sprang up all over the country. Some were simply a lion or a bear in a small cage at the local gas station, while others like the Everglades Wonder Gardens consisted of well thought out animal habitats featuring a wide variety of animal species. These roadside zoos planted the seed that created an interest in wild animals and wildlife conservation that would take root and grow and lead to the development of many of today's larger municipal zoos. Almost all of these small zoos have disappeared, but the Everglades Wonder Gardens has persisted continuing its mission of stimulating an interest in wildlife, educating its visitors and even preserving some species, like the Florida panther, from extinction."

It was twilight when we walked through the fringes of the cypress head, weaving our way through the stand of trees. This head was almost completely dry, just a deep central open pool about thirty-feet across was free of trees except for a few large gnarled pond apple trees on one side of the water and a large clump of tall fire flag on the other. Lester told us this was an alligator hole and the big alligator that lived here had probably fled into its cave, which was up under the pond apple trees, for protection when it heard us coming. Hundreds, if not thousands of frogs leaped into the water or the clumps of emergent fire flags to escape us, and multitudes of small fish occasionally broke the still surface out at the central part of the pool. The ground between the cypress trees was like a carpet; there was no ground cover except short grass that almost looked like it had been mown and cypress knees that were crowned with tussocks of strap ferns. I had waded flooded cypress domes on field trips with Ralph Curtis before but this was my first visit to a dry cypress system — it was almost cathedral-like. Back in 1955 invasive exotic trees like Brazilian pepper and *Melaleuca* hadn't invaded and destroyed native habitats, yet.

So far none of us had seen a snake. Lester said, "Find a place to sit and we'll wait for total dark." We did, and it didn't take long. Just about the time pitch black arrived, a pair of barred owls began to serenade us through the stillness of the tree-lined amphitheater. As we enjoyed the sound Lester spoke up again, "Turn on your headlights and goddamn it you boys be careful of where you step. Just get the big ones . . . spread out." I turned on my headlamp, looked down at the ground, and was astounded. There were cottonmouths everywhere coming out from their unseen hiding places to forage around the margins of the alligator hole. I would literally see hundreds of cottonmouths this night and no harmless water snakes of any kind were found in this system. I hunted selectively and bagged several large snakes that averaged about four-feet in length before Lester announced we had collected enough. He never condoned mass collecting as some commercial snake collectors in later years practiced. I would never see such a dense population of cottonmouths again. However, I once came close about ten years later while in the Fakahatchee Strand with my brother Laban photographing native orchids. Because of the ever-increasing road networks and the traffic they bring, the drainage caused by real estate development of such places as Golden Gate Estates and Port of the Islands ruined the Big Cypress Swamp. The invasion of feral pigs into the former wet systems destroyed small vertebrate animal populations. Wild swine will eat anything that's small enough, including cottonmouths and other snakes. As a result, important snake species have been decimated in the wilderness of the Fakahatchee and the region's small isolated cypress heads and parts of the Everglades.

Chapter 22

The Buck Shack

AT ANY ONE TIME someone other than the Pipers lived on the property. In the late forties, a man from Kentucky arrived in Bonita Springs. He traveled with, and was under the care of, a physician by the name of Bernard Ison, who wintered in Bonita Springs. Just what the connection was between Dr. Ison and his patient is unclear. They may have been connected because they were family. The doctor approached Lester and asked if he had any work that this person could do. He warned Lester that the man had a severe alcohol problem and, although he would have to be watched, he was a hard-working individual. Lester put the man to work and that's how the infamous "Speedy" or "Steve" of the 1950s arrived at Everglades Wonder Gardens.

Speedy proved to be an excellent worker and he stayed on the wagon through the first winter he was there. He was dependable and set a pace for other employees to follow. Speedy would get aggravated and complain to Lester if someone didn't perform well and didn't keep up with him — hence his nickname. When it came time for the doctor to return to Kentucky in the spring, Speedy balked and told Lester he preferred to stay put in Bonita Springs and work for him. Rather than lose this good worker, Lester agreed he could stay on if Dr. Ison agreed, which he did. Speedy had been on his best behavior and had remained sober for months. Lester would build a tiny wooden cabin at the rear of the yard, outside the fence, for Speedy's sleeping quarters. This would not have electric or water and he would have to use the Gardens' public restroom facilities and bathe in the slaughterhouse. The cubicle would have a bed and a table and chair; that was it.

Speedy continued to do well for months, until he and Eddie "Jeff" McCoy, a local black man who worked for Bill and Lester got to drinking — and Speedy ended up joining him for nearly a week-long binge. After that, whenever he was paid, Speedy would spend his cash on liquor and not show up for work for day or two. He was now habitually laying up drunk in his sleeping quarters. Lester felt responsible because he had committed to look after Speedy. He realized that he had to take some drastic actions to keep his part of the bargain. Lester explained to Speedy that he was going to hold his pay back and save it for him and Speedy would take his meals as a regular at the Piper's table. Lester made every effort to keep the man away from the bottle and keep him healthy. It worked most of the time.

Speedy's cabin ultimately became known as "The Buck Shack[59]" in the early seventies, long after he was gone. That name was bestowed on it because through the years single men who were employees at the Gardens often lived there. In the mid-fifties Speedy became ill and had to leave the Pipers. He passed away in 1956, and it would be many years before I learned what his correct name really was. It was Granville C. Cornett, and over fifty years later, during my interview with David Piper, Sr., he recalled Speedy's correct name when we talked about him back in the day.

When Warren Boutchia, fresh from Massachusetts, became an employee of Everglades Wonder Gardens, in 1953, he first tent-camped on the outskirts of Bonita Springs. Without transportation, getting to work was difficult for him and Lester offered Warren a place to pitch his tent at the Gardens. Not long after that, they made some room and he bunked in Bill's old house trailer. This had been stored for years under the pole shed and was currently used mostly for storage. Not too long after he made the move, Speedy left his place and it was offered to Warren. After a little freshening up to the interior, he made the move into the tiny cabin. Warren talked of some of the primitive living he had to endure during those times. He said, "The only way I had to take a bath was to swim in the river or fill the wheelbarrow with water and lather up with lye soap and sit down soaking in it for a while. Then I'd step out and rinse myself off with a hose. I did that about once a week. One time I forgot and left the soapy water in the wheelbarrow overnight and it ate all of the paint off the inside, right down to the bare metal. When he saw that the next morning, Lester wasn't too happy and I had to repaint the wheelbarrow."

Warren remembers another incident related to 1953 sleeping arrangements at Everglades Wonder Gardens, "In the very beginning, when I first started working at Everglades Wonder Gardens, for a short time I lived in my two-man umbrella tent on the backside of the Gardens' property. When Lester hired a new guy who needed a place to stay I invited him to sleep in my tent temporarily. Things went good until a few nights later when I was suddenly awakened in the middle of the night by low voices. A woman was whispering, in a concerned tone, '. . . but he'll wake up.' Then I heard my tent mate answer her in a hushed but nervous voice, 'No, he won't.' He probably didn't care if I did or not at this point. This was happening just inches away from me, with me trying my damnedest to be quiet as the heavy breathing and other passionate sounds of good sex started and became louder and louder. My own heavy breathing was not to convince them of my sleeping condition, but it was because I was trying to stay calm. We all eventually drifted off to sleep and in the morning I was somewhat introduced to the woman. I later made it clear to him that this kind of living arrangement wasn't welcome in my tent."

There were a few strings attached if one stayed in the Buck Shack. Whoever slept there could be jostled out of bed unexpectedly at any hour to accompany Lester and go pick up some errant cow, horse, or mule that wandered into the path of a vehicle or train and had been killed. This was a common event and both the Lee and Collier County Sheriff Department dispatchers called and requested that someone from the Wonder Gardens come and remove the animal that was often blocking the traveled way. And, they wanted it done immediately. This was an unwritten

memorandum of understanding and it served two purposes —
keeping the highways and roadways unobstructed and safe, and a
source of food for hungry mouths. The dead animal would be
trucked back to the Gardens and usually butchered right away so
the meat would not spoil. The quarters of meat were hung in a
spacious walk-in cooler. Other body parts were stored in containers
in the same refrigeration unit and all would later be used as food for
the captive carnivores.

There was one other string attached to the shack. When
Lester was asked to furnish animals for exhibits at the Southwest
Florida Fair and the Florida State Fair he usually responded by
trucking a group of caged animals to the function. He also trucked
an unmarried employee along with the wildlife, to care for the
specimens while they were at the Fair and that employee was
customarily the resident of the Buck Shack. The Fair jaunts were
the only paid vacations anyone who worked at Everglades Wonder
Gardens ever got.

Mrs. Anna May Piper, the family matriarch, arrived in
Bonita Springs to stay, in 1945. About a year prior to this, Bill and
Lester bought a small vacant cottage for their mother and moved it
onto the front of the property across the driveway from the entrance
building. It was renovated and ready to become Mrs. Piper's
residence. Originally, the cottage was located outside of the
perimeter fence. After the restaurant was built a few years later,
Anna May Piper's residence would be about equidistant between
the Gardens' entrance and the restaurant.

In 1948, Lester, Lucille, David and a playmate of his, John
Trew, and Lester's mother took a bus trip north to Detroit. After
arriving there, Lester bought a new Studebaker stake-body truck,
complete with a hydraulic-lift tailgate, and a high canvas topped
bed. He also bought a new Plymouth sedan to tow home to Florida
behind the truck. While in Wyandotte, he arranged the sale of all
of his remaining real estate. Then he loaded the rest of his mother's
and his and Lucille's belongings in the car and truck and made the
return trip to Florida nonstop; other than food, fuel, and pit stops.
From all available evidence, the man would never leave the state of
Florida again. When Lester first arrived in Bonita Springs to stay,
in 1936, he drove a Model-A Ford sedan. The last automobile he

owned, and rarely drove, was an early fifties model Pontiac sedan. He would use it on special occasions, but for the most part it was stored in the pole shed next to Bill's old trailer. Lester would drive pick-up trucks for the rest of his days, after the big Studebaker truck had seen its last days on the road.

The Piper brothers would never admit it, but they soon regretted they had brought their mother south because Anna May Piper made them tow the line, and their lifestyles would at times be hampered to complete frustration. As the years passed, Bill usually stayed clear of the place preferring not to be around too long and end up under the domination of his mother. He had built a comfortable home on two lots situated in the northwest corner of the property that was accessible on Baxter Street so he could avoid going near his mother in the event he had a few of his favorite mixtures — Pepsi Cola and gin.

After her arrival, Mrs. Piper took over most of the domestic duties in Lester and Lucille's household. She prepared most of the meals, and eventually ruled the roost. She frowned on her son Lester's occasional enjoyment of a few drinks at the end of the day. In fact she had a belligerent attitude about drinking alcohol. In 1956, Naples resident and teenager Richard Beatty was a frequent volunteer at the Gardens on weekends. During an interview he recalled the following episode, "Charles LeBuff, Lester, and I were putting the roof on the new golden eagle cage. It was really hot up there and Lester got thirsty and needed a drink. After his successful surgery for throat cancer in 1955 his salivary glands didn't work properly, so he had to sip water or some other liquid fairly regular. Lester went inside the pole shed and Charles and I started to go inside the store to buy ourselves some sodas out of the machine, when all of a sudden we heard Lester scream from the tool shed, 'Son of a bitch!' He repeated this phrase and then added a few more choice words. I thought some animal must have escaped, and then I thought, maybe he had been snake bitten. We ran to him and with a big grin on his face, he said, 'Look what I found!' He showed us a bottle of his favorite rye whiskey, and continued, 'I hid this from my mother about six months ago. Go get us some Seven-Ups.'

"We went into the slaughterhouse to have a few drinks. It seemed okay with Lester when we poured some of his whiskey into our soda bottles, but I think he was watching how much we drank and he was ready to put a stop to it before we had too much. We were standing at the butcher table and were tipping them back when Lester's mother came in unexpectedly. I handed the bottle of whiskey to Charles and he pushed it over in front of Lester. Mrs. Piper started yelling and beating Lester with her cane as she reprimanded him about the evils of drinking. I learned then and there that a man is never too old to get his ass whipped by his mamma. Lester was in his mid-fifties and his mother in her late seventies. Then and there I also learned to say yes ma'am to her."

Mrs. Piper had a blood disorder. According to her grandson David she had frequent bouts with excessive bleeding. I recall one time she had to be hospitalized in 1956 and Lester mentioned she would have to have blood transfusions. I went to the blood donor center in Naples on my day off and I gave a pint of my blood for Mrs. Piper. I thought I understood that it would be credited to her account. She was released from the hospital, and sometime later I was helping Lester bone some horsemeat. We were standing at the butcher table cutting meat off of the huge bones when he suddenly broke into a rant, "Charlie, I know you donated some blood for my mother . . . Bill and me really appreciate that. Those sons of bitches at the Naples Hospital sent me a bill and they charged me $35.00 each for the five pints that people like you donated to her. I don't know where in the hell they got the nerve to do that, but I'll damn sure find out!" I never heard anymore on the issue.

Mrs. Piper passed away in July of 1959. After that her cottage remained vacant and fell into disrepair. A concrete solar screen fence was erected between it and the parking lot. The building was used for storage until Lester decided it would replace the Buck Shack and be used for a staff member to live on site for additional security. Ken Morrison would live in the cottage for several years and as Lester aged Ken would become his sidekick and front line of security — his buffer against invasion of his privacy that he had started to yearn for as the years advanced.

Chapter 23

Lester, the Intimidator

THROUGH THE YEARS BILL Piper was the public persona of the partnership with his brother Lester. If any member of the public had a fleeting moment of personal contact with one of the famous Piper brothers it was common that even thirty or forty years later for that person to publicly state, "I knew Bill, or Lester, Piper." Some people who had minor business dealings with them found it easy to say, "Bill Piper was a friend of mine." These statements are not true, because the interpretation of the event was self-perceived. It took very special circumstances to become friends with either of these men, and very few individuals who got close enough to shake their hands would pass the test or make the grade and be allowed into their inner circle. During their early adult careers they had quickly learned it was unwise to trust anyone and they were never really able to shake off that fundamental perception of human nature.

Bill had more experience in the ways of the world than Lester because of his time in the Navy and his acquaintances and business contacts around Lee and Collier counties. Bill's ability to communicate with people was definitely broader than his younger brother's. Lester simply didn't like people in general and managed on a high level of expertise to be able to keep them outside of his chosen inner circle. He also preferred to remain in the background when it came to routine business issues, unless it dealt with actual money, and he relied on brother Bill to make most decisions. Lester wouldn't always agree with his brother, and as any employee can attest their arguments could become loud and testy. Lester wanted to be left alone to do the things he did best and enjoyed the most in life — caring for and appreciating his animals. Lester was an introvert and Bill was just the opposite. Bill was the showman of the pair and anyone who was ever around them in a work setting will attest Bill was the boss. When Bill branched out to become a fulltime cowman, Lester assumed management of Everglades Wonder Gardens, but for years into the future it was Bill's name that the public attached to operation of the attraction.

On February 25, 1954, Bill and Lester Piper purchased several sections of land at a place called The Mule Pens out in Collier County. Bill started to improve pastureland there and leased two sections to farmers who cleared the land to raise crops. When the farming lease expired, Bill and his nephew, David, graded and configured the surface and turned it into some fine-looking pasture. Bill eventually had over three hundred-head of cattle on the land he and Lester owned, and later he leased more pasture near Cape Coral. The operation of the ranching activities eventually became a contentious subject between the brothers. Costs for stock, fences, structures, laborers, seed, feed, fertilizer, taxes, and ongoing improvements were met from the income of the Everglades Wonder Gardens. In the late fifties, after a few after-work nips of Old Overholt, Lester would often complain to his regular audience, his friends and Gardens employees, "Bill has never sold a goddammed cow[60]."

His older brother never intimidated Lester; he would go toe to toe with Bill anytime he had to. He seemed to fear his mother's wrath, but there were times that Lester was intimidated by someone other than his mother. The one character that always frightened him was a U.S. Game Management Agent[61] by the name of Jake Wolfley. Jake Wolfley lived in Orlando and periodically telephoned to be sure Lester would be present on a certain date. Then he would announce he would be visiting to conduct an inspection on that day. Lester was the permit holder and he had to be present, hence the advance notification. Wolfley, a federal law enforcement agent, was the field administrator who made sure that migratory bird permittees were conforming to their permit restrictions as granted by the U.S. Fish and Wildlife Service before a permit would be renewed. Lester always knew right off the top of his head if he had more species, or specimens of each, than his permit allowed. I remember him acting like he was in a near-panic mode one afternoon when a few of us were at the butcher table at lunchtime. He told one of the crew, "After you finish eating go out to the bird pens and catch the two purple gallinules and put them in a small box and take them over to Bill's for a couple of days. Don't forget they're there when you feed that side of the yard either." These beautiful birds had been brought into the Gardens from a resident at Port Royal, in Naples, who was sure the parents had abandoned the chicks. The two handsome birds were now grown, but they were not listed on the permit. Supposedly, at least Lester thought so, Jake Wolfley who in Lester's words, "went by the book," would frown — maybe even enough to revoke a permit — if he should find an unlisted species at the Gardens. Even though the two purple gallinules could simply have been administratively included and noted as orphaned being held for rehabilitation and eventual release, Lester wasn't willing to go there. He wasn't taking any chances because Jake Wolfley always talked tough and Lester correctly read his personality. You could tell that Lester respected him because he was a straight shooter.

Bill Piper often was a regular customer at Baird's bar at the end of the day. Most of the patrons were locals, but occasionally out-of-towners came in for liquid refreshment. Two independent parties told me of an altercation the Piper brothers once had in the early days at Bairds[62]. One night, Bill got into a brawl with a small group of men and they were steadily getting the best of him as he continued to defend himself. It got out of hand when one of the men left and went outside. He decided it was time to bring a firearm into the four against one fray, and walked back in with a shotgun.

One of the regular patrons who knew Bill saw what was going on. Once the fistfight started, he went to the Gardens and called Lester out and told him his brother was in trouble, he was being ganged up on. Lester leaped over the Gardens' fence and made a beeline for Baird's and got there about the time the shotgun became part of the mix. This didn't deter Lester and he jumped right into the fight alongside his brother. He managed to grab and get the weapon away from the person that was armed. Then Lester took the shotgun out of the building. There was a large pole outside the tavern and Lester put the gun on the other side of the pole, and then reached around with both hands. He grabbed the end of the barrel with one hand and the stock in the other, and pulled back on them. Lester was a powerfully strong man, and he would continue to be, even well after he had reached his prime. From all accounts it was without much effort he wrapped the barrel around the pole, ruining the gun. With that threat out of the way, Lester then went back inside and joined his brother. Together they finished the brawl and cleaned all the tough guys out of the bar in short order.

Lester Piper could be very difficult to work for at times . . . well, almost all of the time. He was centered in his daily routine and expected one hundred ten percent out of every employee at all times until the work was finished. When it was done, it was usually time to relax and partake in a little fellowship. The care of the animals came first in Lester's view, as it should. In the evenings after a long day and after all the employees had left for the day, Lester would often sit in a chair on the front porch near the entrance door. Lucille would sometimes join him and together they would relax, enjoying the night air while watching the traffic move along the Trail. Lester Piper didn't mince his words; he always came right out and said what was exactly on his mind. Like the time he unexpectedly admonished young Dennis Morgan when they were on a repair job in the yard early one morning. Out of the clear blue, Lester said, "Well, I seen you last night, Morgan. You'd drive from one end of town to the other. You'd go down to the Dome, turn around and come back by and go to the Beach Road and turn around. You'd come back every ten or fifteen minutes. All you're doing is driving around looking for something to stick your dick in."

Dennis Morgan chuckled when he recalled another tidbit of Lester's humor that he overheard during his time at the Gardens. "We were cleaning out the otter pen and it wasn't too long after I started work at the Wonder Gardens. We had drained the pen for the night and several of us were down inside with stiff brushes removing the algae build-up from the bottom and walls, the parts that were underwater during the day. We didn't do this every night, just when the algae got real bad. We'd have to spray the otters with the hose to keep them back while we scrubbed the concrete. I was down in there scrubbing for the first time, and I was afraid of them because they would sneak up on us while we worked and would try to bite us. Lester was standing watching us work, and from his expression I could tell he had already had his third large glass of Old Overholt for the day and was kind of getting a little glow on. The last of the people from the final tour of the day were women and they had to walk by the otter pen to reach the exit. One of the panthers in a cage near the otter pen was in heat and had been screaming and screaming for a while. Another panther in one of the cages in the back of the yard chimed in and seemed to be answering the one near us. The girls stopped and one of them looked at Lester, and said, 'What's wrong with that panther? Is it in pain?' She asked the question with a tone that sounded like we weren't taking care of it. I looked at Lester . . . I could see the gears turning . . . he said, 'Well let me tell you Ma'am, this panther's pants are on fire and she wants that one back there to come over and put it out for her. You know what I mean, Ma'am?' The woman who asked the question blushed and a shocked look came over her face. She and her friends walked off and Lester looked down at us and winked and gave one of his sly devilish grins."

After you had been trained and learned your duties and performed them to Lester's standards you seldom would fall out of his good graces. It was when someone didn't perform or did something so far out of line that Lester Piper exploded. Everyone within range was fair game for his anger. It was simple to read the elements of his mood. If you heard metal pans bouncing around inside the slaughterhouse, you should be smart enough to stay clear, go back out in the yard, make another round, and clean animal cages again until things quieted down.

Ralph Curtis often talks about a day in 1953 when Lester had to leave for a couple of days on a business trip. He was going to attend an out-of-town meeting of the Florida Attractions

Association. Everglades Wonder Gardens was one of the earliest members of this state-wide group and their meetings were one of the few things that would get Lester motivated enough to leave the Gardens for any length of time. Ralph tells about what happened after Lester left. "Don Carroll was off work this particular day and Lester sort of left me in charge of the crew, but before he left he told Warren Boutchia to trim the grass around the flamingo pool. Those were all the instructions that he gave Warren about the work project. The runners of the Saint Augustine grass had crept over the concrete edge of the pool. Some of the grass was in the water and didn't look very attractive. Warren got started with an edging tool, a rake, a hoe, and a wheelbarrow. He began removing the densely matted grass from the circumference of the large shallow pool. Each time I passed with a group I watched his progress, but I didn't pay too much attention because I was sure Lester had told him exactly how he wanted the trimming job done.

"The next day Warren was back on the job and finished up the flamingo yard project. When Lester got home later in the day I was guiding near the flamingos and I happened to see and hear Lester's reaction to "Butcher's" trimming job . . . we knew Warren by the nickname of Butcher in those days. Lester was near one of the gates of the pen and holding on to the branch of a tree — just hanging there limply and shaking his head and muttering to himself. Warren had removed a swath of perfectly good grass from an area about three feet wide all the way around the pool. When he saw me Lester lit in to me about it, right in front of the people I was guiding, 'How in the hell did you let him go ahead and do that?' After he blew his top I told him straight out that he never told me how he wanted it done. If I remember correctly Warren was never reprimanded by Lester — he liked him, and the grass soon grew back in and repaired the bald strip of dirt."

If Lester liked you he didn't often express it very well. As an example, Dennis Morgan remembers, "I was working with Lester on the roof of the eagle cage and I told him that me and Carl Williams were going into the Army under the buddy program, and that next week we were going to Miami to get our physicals and whatever. He waited a while and didn't say too much but I could see the wheels moving. Pretty soon he said, "Well Morgan, let me tell you this — if they don't keep you, don't come back here, because if you're too goddammed sorry that the Army won't take you I don't think I want you back!' I knew that he and I were friends and it probably bothered him I was leaving. I think it was just a matter of pride, I'm sure I could have gone back."

Photo courtesy of Ken Morrison.
Used by permission of David Piper, Jr.

A happy Lester Piper, circa 1956. His grandson, David Piper, Jr. has this portrait of Lester tattooed on his forearm.

Ralph Curtis, looking back at his Everglades Wonder Gardens experiences, shared the following; "I came down to Bonita Springs with some other people from the Hillsborough County Herpetological Society in Tampa, in early 1952. There was an older fellow by the name of Ernest Taylor who was the president of the group. He kept it all together. I wrote him from Illinois and inquired if anyone would be making a trip into the Everglades any time soon. A couple of friends and I wanted to do some snake collecting in the Everglades and wanted to know if anyone was going to plan anything now that summer was coming. It turned out that Ernest Taylor himself was planning such a trip. The Pipers had contacted him, and some other people had contacted the Audubon Society up in Tampa that he was a member of — about the giant cypress out in The Corkscrew. The Lee Tidewater Lumber Company was cutting timber near there back in the early fifties and if something wasn't done soon they would wipe out the rest of the big trees. There was just a little patch of the really old and big trees remaining and they were in The Corkscrew. The Pipers were worried, the state was worried, and Mr. Taylor was going down there to do a biological survey. I started corresponding with him about going along on the survey and he let me know that he was all in favor of us going along. So, my two friends and I in Illinois made plans to go along with him. There was also a woman going that was a freelance magazine writer and a man who was a photographer. We made our plans and got all of our equipment together after Mr. Taylor told us what we should bring along. He was going to furnish transportation from Tampa after we got that far. We were to gather at Everglades Wonder Gardens in Bonita Springs. That would be our base, because Bill Piper was really interested in the project Ernest Taylor was promoting to save The Corkscrew from destruction. While we were at the Gardens, Don Carroll and someone else were moving about a six-foot crocodile from one pen to another. Don was holding this thing while standing on top of the pen wall and everybody was standing back watching him. He needed someone to take it long enough so he could get off the wall. I stepped forward to help along with the regular worker. We took it from him, and Don jumped down off the wall. I found out that Don was an ex-serviceman . . . not a Marine like I was, but he had been in the Army, so we seemed to connect right off. In the process of helping with the crocodile I asked him, 'Is there any chance of getting a job here?' My wife Billye was expecting our first child and I wasn't making enough money working in the gas station up in Illinois. She was working as a secretary and her income was going to be cut off once our baby arrived. Don said, 'I don't know, I'll talk to Lester about it.'

Ralph Curtis, 1953, during a break from guiding, playing with a bottle-nursed Florida panther kitten. This cat is a yearling and its juvenile spots are still faintly visible.

"We went into the Glades with a Florida Game Warden by the name of Ray Barnes. We set up camp and he'd drive us around in his Jeep in the daytime and then he'd go back home at night. He'd come back out the next morning and pick us up and we'd go somewhere else to look around. We walked into where the big cypress dome was and waded around the edges of Lettuce Lake. Ernest Taylor was constantly taking photographs. He was shooting slides with his 35-mm camera. I wound up going back to Illinois to pack up and return to Bonita Springs in short order. Lester Piper had told Don Carroll to hire me as a guide.

"I'd worked there for a few months and thought I was doing a pretty good job. I asked Lester, 'Can I talk to you?' He said, 'Okay' as he was washing and throwing feed pans around, and I said, 'I'd like to have a raise.' All of a sudden the feed pans are banging around again, but this time louder. He starts pulling his whiskers and tugging on his hat. He stopped, then replied, 'Goddammed people come here and they want to work because they love animals so much. First thing you know they want a vacation, time off, and a raise. If you paid someone to screw, I'll be damned if they wouldn't want some time off . . . a raise, and all the rest. I don't know . . . how much do you want?' I wasn't sure what I was going to ask for and I said, 'About a nickel an hour.' He came back with, 'This ain't all my business you know. I have a partner. There's two of us — Bill's my partner and I have to ask him.' I almost said, Oh, forget it, but I didn't. I just walked off.

"The next day he started to walk by me and suddenly stopped. I was doing something, either guiding or washing down an animal cage. He said, 'Bill said to give you a quarter more an hour!' A quarter more an hour . . . I'd only asked for a nickel."

Ralph enjoyed reminiscing about his time at Everglades Wonder Gardens, and continued talking about the pay scale. "I got in big trouble one time over how much money I made. One time Harry Metz and I got into a discussion about money. He asked me, 'How much do you make an hour?' I wouldn't answer him because Lester had always told me not to talk about how much he paid me. Harry wouldn't let up, and he said, 'Well, I'm doing pretty good. I know I'm making more than you are.' He wouldn't quit, he just kept going on and on about money. He asked me again, 'How much money do you make? You sure I'm making more than you?' He wouldn't let up and I shouldn't have done it, but I told him how much I was making. The next day, Lester walks up and jumps all over me. 'I told you what you make and what the other people here make is none of anybody else's business. You said something to Metz and now he wants more money. I already told you what you make is between me and you!'"

I arrived in Bonita Springs in late 1952. Don Carroll had been a friend of my father's when Don was young. He was one of my father's helpers. At about the time my folks started making plans to leave the Boston area, Don and his wife and son came north to see his parents and siblings and Don and Jackye stopped by our house for a visit. After my folks heard Don's stories about

Bonita Springs, that was where they ultimately decided our family would relocate. I first met Lester Piper in 1952, and by early 1953 he had given me a part-time weekend job as a fill-in guide. After I graduated from high school in 1954, I went to work at the Gardens on the full-time schedule and I would remain as primary guide until nearly the end of 1956. My younger brother, Laban, had joined the Gardens' full-time work force by 1956. My job was beginning to deteriorate by this time. Lester and Bill's brother-in-law had started to work at the Wonder Gardens. He was a classic know-it-all kind of guy; one who had mastered every aspect of any position in which he had ever been employed. If you didn't believe that, you just had to ask and he'd tell you that he had. He often bragged that he was a "master mechanic," but in reality he couldn't figure out how to lay out and cut a compound miter. He was also known for the absolute fact that he had never made a mistake. Whenever he was around Lester, his personality would change and he'd slyly try to find an opening to degrade anyone on the staff, or their work. It seemed to me he was obsessed with the need to receive Lester's adoration, and Lester seldom conveyed it. I'm sure, in reality, Lester knew that his sister's husband was a backstabber and everyone around him knew it. But Lester was between a rock and a hard place — this guy was "family." I'd have to work with him from time to time and together we built two pole sheds, one an extension of the one at the Gardens and another out in the Piper brothers' Bonita Springs pasture. I also worked with him on the construction of a large display cage for an Andean condor and two golden eagles[63]. I had already learned how the man operated so I was always careful what I said about anything around him and I did my job, as I perceived it should be done. His antics kept the pot well mixed and morale among my coworkers at Everglades Wonder Gardens plummeted to an all-time low — especially on the rare occasions when Lester seemed to side with him and accept his input on some issue about one of the staff. Although Lester had never seriously reprimanded my brother and me, we decided we didn't want to continue to work for Lester any longer under such contentious conditions.

All we had to do was break this news to Lester Piper. This chore was left up to me, but I hesitated because I knew how Lester reacted when a worker he liked left, and my brother Laban and I both did our jobs well. Lester couldn't ever bitch about our job performance. Although we thought it best to give some kind of a notice, I dragged my feet and told Laban to standby. We'd make our move when conditions warranted it — we had given ourselves a window of about one week before beginning a new job we each had accepted, but the clock was ticking. And, I was totally afraid to act — because I feared the inevitable clash with Lester. When riled up, Lester Piper was a very intimidating personality. I had seen it all before when others he liked left without giving notice and exiting on good terms.

The right moment presented itself a few nights later. It was nearly dark when Lucille Piper let the last group of paying customers into the Gardens. I don't know how she expected me to give them anything close to their money's worth for a Garden's tour in the remaining minutes of daylight — they really couldn't see much as the cages and pens grew darker. I had no choice but to hurry. The customers knew that's what I was doing, so they became vocally upset with the management, and me. They were told it was they who had insisted on entering near dusk and I was just trying to help them see the wildlife. When I was finished I went inside the slaughterhouse to get my lunch container and Laban, who was hanging around waiting for me, to start home. The Piper brother-in-law was in the building cleaning up the butcher table after the meat for the panthers had been prepared, and Lester was out in the yard personally feeding his big cats. The master mechanic made some smart-ass, off the wall remark about my attitude, because he overheard me telling Laban I was ticked off because I was forced to do a tour until dark. That's all it took, and when I told him where to shove his opinion, an intense and very loud argument broke out between us. About that time, Lester's mother walked through the door into the fray. She stood there listening to us with her hands on her hips and an evil unmotherly expression across her face. Then, jumping in to support her son-in-law's side of the issue, Mrs. Piper spoke, "If these boys don't like their jobs they can go ahead and quit!" That's all it took, and out the door I went — looking for Lester.

I found him crouched down at his panther's cage near the otter pen. He was tossing chunks of meat underneath the access flap at the front of the cage as the cat paced back and forth, purring loudly. I knew he saw me shaking as I cleared my throat and said, "Lester, Laban and I are quitting tonight. You can ask your mother why." I started to turn away, and all hell broke loose. Lester began throwing empty metal feed pans and buckets around in a frenzy. They were bouncing off the concrete and wire with resonating clanging sounds. He wasn't saying anything during all of this, just reacting to my words. I had never seen Lester so mad before and it was scary. I backed away from him, turned around to go get Laban and get in my car and leave before it got any worse. All I could think of was that he was about to grab me and then pick me up over his head and throw me in the crocodile pen. As I left him fuming in his temper tantrum, he yelled at me, "Go ahead and quit, but you'll be back!" I turned and stomped off as I silently scoffed at his comment, but he would prove to be a fortune-teller.

Lester was right on. I asked him for my job back less than a year later and went back to work at the Everglades Wonder Gardens the first week of 1958. Conditions were much better. The master mechanic was gone. The scuttlebutt was that Lester and Lucille and he and Anna Mae had recently dined at a popular North Naples barbecue restaurant. As they were leaving, Lester caught him in the act of stealing the waitress' generous tip that he had personally left on the table. The word was that it had ended up in a nasty scene when Lester started raising hell with his sneaky brother-in-law. Although guilty beyond a reasonable doubt, Anna Mae's husband took offense and shot off his mouth, and was now a persona non grata at Everglades Wonder Gardens. Good riddance!

The more I was around him, the more I realized that Lester Piper lacked good employer skills and was very demanding of us all. None of us could keep up with Lester's tough and demanding work ethic. However, he did a great job of managing to balance the crew to a level just above complete disgruntlement with his frequent displays of humor and generosity, and high level of fairness. At the end of the workday his attitude would change for the better after he had downed a few belts of Old Overholt rye whiskey or a few cans of Ballantine Beer or Silver Bar Ale, his favorite beverages. I soon discovered he viewed my work on a different plane than my coworkers. When I was guiding, I was less impacted with work-related pressures because of his mood swings since I wasn't working directly under his thumb like the others. I watched many new workers leave his employ after only a few days on the job. Lester was only fifty-two years old in 1954; he was in his prime — powerfully strong and untiring and mean, but I don't remember him ever firing anyone. His tactic to get rid of someone he didn't like was to constantly reprimand and ridicule the worker, and make his work experience so miserable he would leave voluntarily. I once stood nearby and heard Lester launch into a tirade against someone he was unhappy with, someone he wanted to make quit, to run-off, and he verbally degraded the employee's father so severely the poor worker was so insulted that he stormed off the premises in tears. Some men that quit under such circumstances may have wanted to react differently, but they weren't brave enough to stand up to Lester's rage and take a poke at him. I'm sure that if anyone had tried that, it would have been the major mistake of an abbreviated life. We who worked there knew the crocodiles were always hungry.

After one occasion we were all quite sure that an employee Lester had recently run off by such a rude personal assault made an attempt to get even. I had to be at work by seven o'clock in the morning, even though the door didn't open for business and tourists didn't enter until eight. I was responsible for specific duties. First, I had to remove the burlap bags on which the otters had dried their fur the previous night, and then rinse all areas of their concrete pen. Then, I opened the valve that started to fill their pen with fresh water because it had to be kept completely dry overnight. Next, I would move to the nearby panther cages and with hose pressure, loosen and direct their excrement so it would wash down the drain. I'd check the harmless snake pit for any overnight mortalities and then move over to review the well-being of those inhabitants of the small crocodilian pen, and finally inspect the alligator snapping turtles and "Big Joe," the immense but toothless Florida American crocodile. Meanwhile, my coworkers were doing similar work; cleaning, raking, and washing cages in their designated work areas. With all else done, I'd get a supply of dry towels to clean the few glass-front cages and wipe all the pit railings dry throughout the Gardens, so early customers wouldn't get wet from the dew that rested on them. I was then ready and standing by to begin the first tour.

After arriving at work on this particular morning, I went into the small building where we butchered horses and cows and prepared their meat and organs for the carnivores' diets. I put my lunch inside a large upright refrigerator and headed for the yard. About the time I exited that building and reached the gate leading into the yard, I heard a terrified shriek ring out. When I opened the gate, just in front of me stood Bill and Lester's mother, Anna Piper. She had just stepped out of the family kitchen and was standing, frozen. She was afraid to move and was glaring at an eight-foot long crocodile on the concrete walk between the two of us. I looked and saw that the gate of the alligator and crocodile pen, which housed that size class, was standing wide open. Someone who had a key had unlocked the padlock and most of the crocs and gators had made their escape during the night. This pen was where I assembled customers to start each tour.

At the sound of his mother's screaming, a half-dressed and shoeless Lester pushed open the door of the kitchen, stepped outside, and swung into action. About fourteen alligators and crocodiles had taken advantage of this rare opportunity and made an escape. Lester maneuvered around the croc and went into the pole shed for a line and a pole. He lassoed the irritable crocodile and we dragged it toward the pen from which it had fled. It was strong, twisting and turning, and fighting us with brute force, but it was soon back in the enclosure. The pole was then used to loosen and remove the loop from around the croc's neck. Lester's son David and coworker Herb Priddy, who had just arrived for work joined us. The Gardens' doors didn't open until late that morning, postponed until after we had scoured the grounds and recaptured all the escapees. It was fortunate that the perimeter pole fencing surrounded the yard. Soon all of the temporarily free crocodilians were back in their enclosure and things returned to normal. I'm sure Lester had a good idea of who had opened the lock, but nothing further was ever said.

On December 15, 1958, I told Lester Piper that I would be leaving his employ on the twenty-seventh. I had been accepted for a position with the U.S. Fish and Wildlife Service on Sanibel Island and I would move there on the twenty-eighth. A few weeks before giving him my notice I had already introduced Lester to my friend George Weymouth. George was a very knowledgeable naturalist, eager for a full-time job in the wildlife field, and he wanted to fill my position. Because I had given an appropriate notice and Lester had a replacement for me, I left the Everglades Wonder Gardens the second time with Lester's best wishes for a great future. Even though he was a rough and tough man and he usually intimidated me because of his low anger threshold, I would fully admire and respect him for the rest of his, and my, life.

By the time I arrived at the Gardens, Bill Piper wasn't around much. He would come in near our quitting time after he had worked out in the pasture all day. It was customary that most evenings he'd make a brief appearance, go and say hello to his mother, and then come into the slaughterhouse and say a few words to his brother and anyone within earshot. Then he'd go into the grain shed and scoop out a big pan full of Miller's kibbles from a barrel for his cow dogs and walk back to his house to feed them. I worked with him a few times in the pasture over the years and I remember Bill taught me how to milk a cow, one of those times. Whenever I rode along with Bill, he enjoyed talking about wildlife and his experiences with the bears. I also managed to get considerable information out of him about crocodiles; that is, once I got him talking.

George Weymouth shares another side of Bill's otherwise tough persona," One day I was cleaning the slanted glass on the rattlesnake pit, when all of a sudden I heard a yell and turned around to see what was going on and I saw Bill running across the yard. He stopped and jumped up on the rail of the long, roof-covered pit that contained alligators, caimans, and crocodiles. Bill stood on the narrow railing, got his balance, and then leaped out and caught hold of an overhead joist that held up the metal roof over the pit. He dangled there for a few seconds and then dropped down among all the crocodilians. I had no idea of what was going on, but unknown to me at the time, a pair of Carolina wrens had nested in Bill's backyard and fledged some chicks. Bill had been following the birds around and was having fun watching them as they learned to fly. I learned later that he thought he had seen one of "his" baby wrens drop into the crocodilian pit as it struggled to learn to fly. The crocodilians weren't full-grown, but they were sizeable enough to be dangerous. But still, not every guy would have had the nerve to do it!"

Chapter 24

Jones Comes "Jonesing" For Dough

THROUGH THE YEARS, SOME of their old cronies from the Detroit River days would show up unexpectedly at the Gardens. Many of these men were down and out and were in need of, and looking for, some money — a grubstake. Lester sometimes took them aside, told them he had no place . . . no room for them, gave them a few bucks to help them out, and then sent them on their way. Others, who he must have liked, were given a job to help them get back on their feet. One of these men was Art Rohmer, Lester's friend from Wyandotte and his sidekick during many hurried crossings of the Detroit River. According to Lester's son, David, his father and Art had a serious disagreement later on, after Art had injured himself on the job at the Gardens. Lester blamed Art's injury on carelessness and apparently wouldn't reimburse him for medical costs. Hearing that, Art threatened that he'd just go ahead and sue Lester for the money to pay his medical bills. Lester jerked Art aside, pulled him up close to his face, and with a growling tone in his voice, Lester said, "Artie, I don't think that would be a very good idea, if you know what I mean." That was the end of that story.

Bill and Lester Piper always operated on a cash basis. Salaries of the Gardens' crew were always paid in cash. When quizzed about that practice by an employee, why they did that rather than make payroll with a check like everybody else, Lester replied, "Because, by God, when I give it to them I want them to be able to spend it right then."

Every financial obligation and purchase of supplies was paid for in cash. I never saw inside Bill Piper's billfold, but I saw the contents of Lester's a few times. The first opportunity was when I went along with him to pick up an old cow that someone wanted to get rid of. Lester and I would trailer it back to the Gardens where it would be slaughtered and butchered and every part of it used for animal food. After the price was agreed on, Lester reached into his pocket and pulled out his very thick wallet. I couldn't believe my eyes. Bills were sorted by denomination and held together with heavy elastic bands — the hundreds alone were nearly a half-inch thick. He pealed off some tens, paid the man, and I led the cow into the trailer.

Ken Morrison once watched a transaction between the brothers, and told me, during an interview, "I was there one evening when Bill came in to pay Lester his share because someone had paid them after they had let them go out on their property and dig out some sabal palms for landscaping. Bill said the total payment was $75.50. I don't know how many trees were involved, but it was probably a hundred, and Bill only paid Lester for twenty-five of them. That's just the way things always seemed to work out between them. Lester didn't have any coins in his pocket to give Bill his change, so he made his brother stand there until he went next door to the store and got the fifty cents to give him exactly the right amount of change.

"This was at about the time they paid $80,000.00 for a brand new Caterpillar front-end loader — all in a stack of bills — cash money! That's just the way those two did business."

Some people who came to see Lester were hoping to score financially. With some of them their intent was obvious, but others were subtler and didn't always have their hand extended with the palm up. Many people approached him indirectly with a handshake as they tried to get their hands into his pockets. Lester could read people remarkably well and knew who to avoid. Some were pushy salesmen, intent on trying to sell him something, but they didn't stay around too long because his brusque demeanor would send them packing.

There were acquaintances of his who thought, at least once, that they had a good chance to separate the man from some of his cash. Ken Morrison told me of one such experience where he was present and heard the whole presentation. It happened back in the early seventies. According to Ken, "I was cutting up mangos and it was about six o'clock . . . maybe a little bit after, and I heard these people pull up in a car in front of the gate. I went out and opened the gate and looked down the driveway. There's a car sitting there and a little old bald short man gets out of the car and turns around and looks at me. I noticed he had a salt and pepper mustache. He said, 'I'm here to see Lester Piper.' I answered him, and said, 'Could I tell him who's calling on him?' 'Tell him its Arthur Jones.' I said, 'Arthur Jones?' 'Yeah, he knows me; I'm in the animal world.'

"I told him to wait, and I walked in and went to the kitchen door, knocked, and said, 'It's me.' Lester told me to come in and I stepped inside the kitchen door. Lucille was just about done putting stuff on the table and he was sitting there with a cup of tea. Seeing this kind of stopped me as I watched his old gnarly hands reach over and put a spoon into a honey jar, spin it real quick, and put it in his tea. I asked myself, 'How the hell did he do that with hands like his?' They were all bent. I said, 'There's a man outside named Arthur Jones. He says he's in the animal business and that you know him.' He said, 'Who?' 'Arthur Jones, he says he knows you.' 'Well, I'm just about to eat. Go out there and walk him around the Gardens. Show him stuff, and about the time you get through I'll be ready to come out.'

"There were two other guys and this one good-looking woman[64] with him. I thought, 'Man this one guy looks familiar.' When we got around to Old Man Mose's pen I told them he was kept by himself because he was nearly perfect, except where someone (or something) had poked one of his eyes out when he was young. Arthur Jones had a barking voice . . . the right in your face kind. He asked, 'Do you know how long he is?' 'Yes, I do, he's twelve-eight.' He said, 'Nope, he's not much over eleven and a half feet long. I learned this by working with alligators and crocodiles. Son, I'll bet you five weeks wages that if we measure that animal he'll be within two or three inches of what I just said.' 'I replied, Really? You can probably afford my wages or four or five times that, but I know how long he is because I measured him.'

"Lester was sitting on the railing of Big Joe the crocodile's pen when we got back. He had on a white T-shirt and was sitting with his arms folded. I asked, 'Are you okay with these people now?' He said he was and we had moved out to the walk leading to the butcher room and I said, 'I've cut up some mangoes and I want to take them out and feed them to the deer.' He said, 'Okay, but come back here in case we need anything.'

"I walked in and picked up the bucket and went back out and walked up to the familiar looking guy and said, 'You know, you look a lot like Dick Butkus[65].' He said, 'I am Dick Butkus.' I said, 'Well that would explain your looks, and I turned around and walked off from him.'

"Arthur Jones told the others they could leave, and he would be done in about and hour and a half. He had a briefcase with him, and also a video setup with a screen. He showed Lester a short film about catching animals in Africa that he was in. It was about forty-five minutes long. Lester was sitting there; I could tell he was not really into it. After the film finished, Arthur Jones said, 'The main reason I came down here is to show you this,' and he sets his briefcase down on one of the glass display cases. 'I just want you to watch this,' and he turns the machine on. It's a commercial with Dick Butkus explaining the Nautilus Workout Machine[66]. He's got this spiel running with Dick Butkus on it, and Lester didn't even know who Dick Butkus is. Arthur Jones continued, 'I'm going around getting people to invest in this and I'll make you a millionaire.'

"Lester looked straight at him and said, 'I'm already a millionaire and I don't need any more investments. That's all I can tell you and that's all I have time for.'

"Arthur Jones picked up his equipment, went back outside where the car was waiting, and he got in and they left."

Chapter 25

Alligators Anonymous

TOURISTS WHO FILLED FLORIDA in the winter, in the days before Disney World had four main things on their mind — sun — oranges — alligators — and, by any means, they wanted to see "pink flamingos," and not necessarily in that or any other particular order. Alligator "farms" and Indian villages displayed the crocodilians along major highways of the southern peninsula, and there were probably more captive alligators in the roadside zoos than there were visible wild ones along the roadways.

The relationship between wild alligators and man in the mid twentieth century was much different than it is today. Alligators were reasonably protected by state regulations in the 1950s, but they continued to be harassed by people and displayed a high level of fear of man. That was wise, because alligators that did not retreat from man usually quickly ended up dead. Whenever human beings entered their habitat, alligators generally fled. Prior to 1948, interactions between alligators and man were so insignificant that no one kept score. That year, the Florida Game and Freshwater Fish Commission began to record the instances of alligator bites and interactions with people, that could best be described as alligator attacks on humans. The more that instances of alligator bites or attacks made the news, the more tourists became fascinated with crocodilians in general. The more alligators that some tourist destination had on display the more likely people were to stop and pay to see that particular exhibit. Everglades Wonder Gardens advertised that their collection contained hundreds of alligators, from hatchlings to giants, and it did. Then if you throw in around a hundred or so American crocodiles of all size ranges, the establishment gave tourists the spectacular exhibit they were looking for.

The Imperial River, at least the part next to Everglades Wonder Gardens, contained many alligators and some of them were very large. These may have been attracted to the vicinity because of the alligator sounds that were being generated by the captives inside the Gardens. The railroad trestle that spans the river just a few yards to the west of the Trail, and a nearby old wooden wharf next to it, was one of Bonita Springs' two major fresh water swimming holes in the fifties. The other was a water control structure several miles to the east of town that every kid in Bonita Springs called "The Dam." During the heat of summer, children were in the water almost continuously during daylight, and some of us even after dark. The wild alligators always kept their distance, but in the reality of today, many of the human population that swam in the Imperial River as kids and survived the alligators will cringe when they think about their dangerous personal exposure; at least I do.

Just in the past decade there have been several deadly alligator attacks on humans in Florida. Things have indeed changed. In the day when alligators and children shared the same aquatic habitat in Bonita Springs the alligators kept their distance. If alligators approached too close to people, they were in range of the human arm, and they were pummeled with stones from the nearby railroad grade. A few stony blows striking their head or back caused the alligators to fear and avoid man. Today, if you throw a stone at an alligator, someone will report you and wildlife officers will view your actions as harassment of an alligator, and charge you with that misdemeanor. With that absurd mindset from officials, the frequency of alligator attacks on humans in Florida will continue to rise.

Alfred Trew helped stock the Bonita Springs Reptile Gardens with many of the first alligators to be caught and put on display. Some of these were nuisance alligators that may have been basking too close to someone's house along the waterways and frightened the homeowner, or they may have preyed on and eaten someone's dog. These alligators were captured by the Piper brothers and ended up as part of their growing collection. Alfred remembered one night, back in 1937, that he was invited to go out with Bill for a night of collecting in his square-stern canoe. They were going to paddle the waters of Oak Creek and look for some little, hopefully just-hatched, alligators. The creek is a tributary of the Imperial River and it also flows underneath the Trail less than a half-mile south of where the river flows. They found a place along the creek where hatchling alligator eyes seemed to be shining everywhere as their battery-powered headlamps panned the marshy shoreline. Alfred said, "We stopped paddling and just drifted to check the place out. We waited for a few minutes, just looking things over. Bill said he didn't see any female guarding them so we started to reach out and picked these little fresh-hatched gators up by the handful. Bill's arms were longer than mine, and he alone caught about thirty of them before we were sure we had them all."

I arrived at work early one morning in 1954 and when I opened the gate my good friend and coworker, Warren Boutchia, met me. He was all excited and told me he had something he wanted me to see. It wasn't quite full daylight yet but I followed him under the pole shed where there was even less light. He stopped and I saw the form of a large alligator on the ground in front of us. It was about eleven-feet long, and it was all trussed up with ropes and its mouth was tied shut. Warren filled me in about this alligator, "I went out with Lester last night and we caught this alligator on the river . . . what a hell of fight that was! As soon as it's light enough I want you to take my picture beside it." I told him I'd be back in about a half-hour when there would be more light under the shed to snap his picture. I put my lunch away and went into the yard to start my morning cage and railing cleaning routine.

When I returned, Warren had his camera all ready. He handed it to me and then he stepped over the alligator's back and stood beside its body and struck a pose. I took the picture and then I said, "Take my picture beside it," as I passed him the camera. We switched places, but before Warren could snap the shutter, and without any warning, I was suddenly and violently knocked off my feet and flat onto my butt by the alligator's powerful tail. It had managed to work its tail loose from the lines during the night and we hadn't noticed the lithe tail was free.

Warren Boutchia and the alligator he helped Lester Piper capture, in 1953. Minutes later, I was knocked to the ground by this animal's powerful tail.

Working with any large alligator or crocodile was always a dangerous and risky business. Many people who routinely handled these powerful animals usually had a sad personal tale to tell, although some of us were lucky and never lost an appendage. Bill Piper's loss of a thumb was a good example of what could happen when things went wrong. One acquaintance of the Piper brothers, Miccosukee Indian Corey Osceola, stood out as an example of a seriously injured alligator handler. Years ago, a large alligator had twisted off Corey's left arm. It happened when he was handling the beast and had lost control. The loss of the arm would one day make this tough Florida Indian famous. In 1958, he would be hired to play the part of Billy One-Arm in the movie, *Wind Across the Everglades*.

Quite often the large bull alligators in the big pen would become belligerent and aggressive with one another. A clap of thunder could sometimes instigate this, or even a loud truck motoring down the Trail, and in minutes a dozen or more of the big brutes would be bellowing. They first would rise slightly and arch their bodies, causing their heads and tails to simultaneously rise out of the water. Then their abdomens trembled with such a vibration that the water beside them seemed to be boiling. This generated a loud bull-like guttural roar as the rush of air exited the alligators' slightly opened mouths. We had to be watchful at such times because quite often two excited bulls would engage in combat. A long factory-made pole was placed nearby to use in the event we had to separate any bulls that engaged one another. Lester instructed each of us, quite emphatically, to always do this from the ground level walkway and not to climb up on the wall and try to part the fighting alligators from there. He always told us, "If anyone ever falls in the big alligator or crocodile pens they're a goner."

Lester Piper didn't always lead his employees by example. He knew it was easier and much quicker to maneuver around the alligator pen if he climbed on top of the narrow concrete cap that ran around the perimeter of the pen. It was a narrow footing along the outside of the inward angled wire and their supports, but he was always careful. He was indeed careful, but age was creeping up and his reflexes weren't quite as good as they once were, nor was his eyesight as keen as it once had been. Lester wouldn't admit any impairment because of such physical changes. Whenever he was nearby and personally responded to fighting alligators, he would grab the pole and hop up on the wall near the place where two bulls were in a tussle. He'd rap the alligators on their boney snouts a few times, or jab them along their exposed sides, and they would usually turn one another loose. Then, defying his own orders, Lester would walk along the top of the wall to the next pair of battling brutes and repeat the separating process, and so on, until all was peaceful inside the pen. Only then would he jump down and go back to whatever he had been doing before the alligator crisis.

Whenever I interviewed someone close to the Piper brothers on a subject germane to this book, one of the questions I always asked him was, "What is the most dangerous thing you ever saw Bill or Lester Piper do?" There were a variety of answers and most of them have been incorporated into the text of this book. For the Piper legacy the Information Highway arrived too late, and there is no library anywhere on this planet that houses information that pertains to the daring lives of the Piper brothers. I didn't have the luxury of just opening a musty filing cabinet in some archival collection and removing an age-stained manila folder to find answers inside it, nor could I search the Internet for a hit that would help me unravel details on what may have been Bill or Lester Piper's most dangerous, perhaps life-threatening episode with wildlife. The experiences of two former employees of Everglades Wonder Gardens do, however, open pathways that uncover first-hand facts that may help answer my question.

We know that as a young man, and again in his middle age, Bill Piper survived two shoot-outs, an attack by a four hundred-pound Florida black bear, a life-threatening snakebite, and a mauling by a bad dog in his old age. These were severe traumatic injuries that men of a lesser constitution may not have survived, regardless of their age. The survivability record of his younger brother, Lester, is much more vague. Not many men would have even attempted to disarm a jittery officer as Lester once did. He received serious bites and scratches over the years, including major snakebites. Lester was exposed to risk on a daily basis, but I can only tell of two very closely-related events where Lester miraculously seemed to avoid certain death. In both cases, American alligators were involved.

Dennis Morgan provides an account that describes what may be the first time that Lester had a major close call with his alligators. It was in the summer of 1958 when this event occurred. Dennis remembers the incident well, and talked about the experience. "One afternoon, Lester sent me to the slaughterhouse for his rye whiskey and Seven-Up. When I returned to the place he and I were working, he wasn't there, but I could hear him calling frantically for me. I kept looking for him until I spotted him inside the alligator pen. He had fallen in and was standing up! When I got there he was pretty far in from the outer wall and he was completely surrounded by big alligators. I passed him a long pole to push the gators away while I opened the gate to let him out. After he got out, he glared at me for a while before chewing me out — for not finding him fast enough! We all had to deal with Lester's hot temper. Just about everyone who was ever lucky enough to work at the Gardens was intimidated by him, but this time he made me mad. I said, 'How would you like it if the next time you call for me, I go to the alligator pen to look for you?' I expected him to throw me in with the gators, but he left without doing anything. Man, was I relieved."

George Weymouth worked as the primary guide at Everglades Wonder Gardens from 1959 until 1963. He shared his recollections of a very similar near calamity involving Lester — as Dennis did with me. "I was guiding and I heard Lester yelling from the direction of the big alligator pool. I ran to the pen to discover that he had fallen in while he was using a pole to break up a fight between two bull gators. At about the time I got there, fellow employee Glen Priddy had already opened the gate to let Lester out. I couldn't believe he was alive and still had all of his extremities. Then I remembered that the evening before, a box full of scrap meat and fat from a local market had been fed to the alligators in the exact corner where Lester had fallen. As he kneeled against the angled wire, and prodded and belted the fighting alligators with a long pole, the fence gave way and Lester had tumbled in on top of the gators. He was wearing a heavy leather jacket because it had cooled off a bit during the night. This probably provided some protection from the biting reaction of the alligators. Lester was likely spared from being twisted into many chunks because the gators were somewhat chilled — or startled, but they were full, too. However, for three days he went ahead laboring steadily on his landscaping project — loading and hauling big loads of dirt around in a wheelbarrow until he finished. Then the word got out. This time he had cracked *two* ribs and only broken *one*. Again, none of the staff was even aware of his injuries! I think no matter how much the man ever hurt, he would never let any of us know about it."

Lester had other work site accidents that were not always wildlife related. George Weymouth shared details with me about another of Lester's injuries, "One day as I walked behind the entrance building, I couldn't help but notice through the Piper's bedroom window that Lucille was wrapping a big elastic body bandage around Lester's barrel chest. Later, I asked her about Lester and she told me that about a week earlier he had fallen off a building he'd built to store grain in and landed, back down, on an empty wheelbarrow. He had cracked one rib and broken two others, yet none of us who worked for him had been informed or had the slightest idea he'd been hurt. Lester had not whimpered or complained once. Of course, he never did!"

Tom Crutchfield first met Lester Piper in 1966, soon after the then teenager had arrived in Lee County from North Florida. Tom would become an internationally known herpetological expert; notably for his extensive work in captive breeding rare species of the world's crocodilians. I interviewed Tom in late 2009, and he fondly recalled some of his interactions with Lester Piper, and respectfully remembers the man as his mentor and friend. He said, "I would visit with Lester at every opportunity and ask him endless questions about crocodiles and other Florida-related herpetological subjects. Lester was an expert who was very close and intimate with everything wild . . . he was a naturalist of the highest order. I'm sure I bored him to tears, but nonetheless he always had time to talk and spend time with me.

"In my opinion Lester Piper was the 'real deal', often imitated but never duplicated. I always thought of him as tough as wet rawhide, and I certainly wouldn't have wanted to be on his bad side. I respected him, was a little afraid of him, and loved him — all at the same time."

Lester would often give guidance, and advise Tom where he might go to locate a particular species he was seeking, one he hoped to observe and perhaps collect those that were new to him. Tom remembered how much he wanted to locate and catch his first indigo snake, but so far he had been unsuccessful. On one collecting trip he stopped in to visit with Lester to get his suggestion as to where he should go to look for an indigo snake. Lester was thinking the question over and in doing so he struck his typical pose, with his head slightly angled and eyes directed down at first. Then he raised his head, wiped his hand across his face, and looked Tom straight in his eyes and said, "You want an indigo snake, huh? Hell, I've got an extra one. You can have it." Tom let him know that he wasn't visiting to ask for a handout; that he would gladly buy the snake from him. Lester's facial expression changed, as he seemed to take offense at Tom's words. He blurted out, "Goddamn it, I'm not in the business of selling snakes. If I want to give you a goddammed indigo snake I'll give the son of a bitch to you!"

A few years later, Tom Crutchfield was managing a wildlife exhibit at the Waltzing Waters attraction in Cape Coral, Florida. He wanted to add a few large alligators to the exhibit so he went to visit Lester, thinking he would possibly be a good source for the alligators without the hassle of getting the permits and then spending time trying to catch wild specimens. Lester let him know up front that he wouldn't sell him any alligators, but said there were a few in the pen that had been injured and were either scarred or were missing parts of their limbs. If he wanted six that were slightly damaged and imperfect, he could have them for free. Lester told Tom, "You'll have to go in the pen and pick them out. Then I'll look them over, and if I want to let you have that particular one, you can go ahead and catch it." This sounded like a good deal to Tom Crutchfield and he told Lester he'd be back the coming weekend with some help.

Tom rounded up some assistance. He called George Campbell, the head of the Southwest Florida Regional Alligator Association, to help. George Weymouth, a former Everglades Wonder Gardens employee, was also enlisted. Both men were considered experienced when it came to working with and handling alligators. At this time, they were involved in managing the nuisance alligator program on Sanibel Island, where they lived. Tom and his helpers arrived at the Gardens on a cold Sunday morning and Lester joined them at the alligator pen.

The plan was to open the tiny gate in the wall of the alligator pen and for Tom to go inside alone. He had to bend down so low he almost had to crawl on his hands and knees to get through the opening and into the water inside the pen. Fog was rising from the surface of the artesian water flowing into the pen because it was much warmer than the ambient air temperature. Tom carefully waded around and inspected and selected the first alligator that he wanted. After Lester approved removal of the specimen, Tom threw a rope over the animal's head, pulled the line snug, and then passed the rope to his helpers on the other side of the gate. He then crawled back through the opening and joined them outside where they all grabbed hold of the rope and pulled the heavy alligator out of the pen. Then, after each one was tied securely, Tom would go back in the pen and pick out another alligator. Not long after they started, a twelve-foot long male was selected and roped, and Tom remembered, "George Weymouth reached over the wall and jabbed the gator with a pole into the side of the animal's gut, thinking it was attacking me and he wanted to divert it. This started a chain-reaction, and either frightened or infuriated the alligator and it charged forward. Its behavior alarmed about half a dozen other alligators near it and they, too, charged ahead at the same time, with me standing directly in their path. I dove out of the way and climbed up on a palm-thatched chickee structure to avoid a toothy collision with over a half dozen charging alligators. When Lester saw this happen, all hell broke loose and he unleashed a verbal assault on George for poking the alligator for what he thought was no good reason."

After things had quieted down, Tom selected a nine-footer. After it was pulled out of the pen and partially secured, he wanted to ascertain the animal's sex, so he performed a digital inspection of the alligator's cloaca. Inserting an index finger into the animal's vent, he palpitated the area, and feeling no penis he declared the specimen a female. Tom continued, "For some reason, George Weymouth must have decided that he wanted to finger an alligator, so he also did an internal probe for sex determination. When he inserted his finger he must have hit a nerve or something else the wrong way, because the alligator swung its head laterally toward me, and in doing so the boney mass struck my leg so hard it nearly broke it. I was in major pain and temporarily out of commission when Lester went ballistic, and he again lashed out and chastised George for nearly causing a serious injury."

As he recounted this alligator episode to me, Tom said, "I learned a wise lesson that day. It taught me to always stay in control, and no matter how experienced someone may claim to be, you must always direct each step yourself when you're working with dangerous animals. Lester Piper already knew that, and he watched me learn that bit of wisdom the hard way."

Chapter 26

Visitors at the Gate

FROM THE TIME THAT the first wildlife specimens were publicly exhibited at Bonita Springs Reptile Gardens, not long after construction first began, and for the lifetime of the Piper brothers' partnership, residents of Bonita Springs were allowed into the exhibit free. This was a courtesy extended to the community by Bill and Lester. To make themselves more noticeable for public recognition, around 1950 the Piper brothers decided they would grow and sport beards as part of their standout public persona. Generally, beards weren't in vogue during mid-twentieth century. Bill grew the first one. It was a goatee, but by the time the movie *Shark River* was filmed, his whiskers had developed into a full beard. Lester opted for a goatee and, once he grew it, he liked his appearance and he would never shave it off. Bill remained mostly clean-shaven after 1958, although he wore a beard from time to time. As Lester aged, he chose to color his beard. We employees used to joke, behind his back of course, that Lester used black shoe polish to maintain his youthful appearance. The truth was that Lucille periodically dyed his goatee while he sat in the kitchen with a towel wrapped around his upper body. By the late 1970s, Lester had abandoned this appearance adjustment and let his goatee go natural.

Through the years many notable people came through the gate at the Gardens. A few entered and left incognito, while others introduced themselves to Bill and Lester because they shared a commonality of interest in wild animals. Marjorie Harris had been born in Boston, but arrived in Bonita Springs at three years of age, in 1918. She and her parents lived on the south side of town. By the time the Pipers arrived, she was already an entrenched and knowledgeable naturalist. By the time construction started on Bonita Springs Reptile Gardens, Marjorie had already left Bonita Springs to attend what is now Florida State University in Tallahassee, from which she graduated in 1936 with a B.S. in zoology. She became a federal wildlife technician and was based near Welaka, Florida. On a trip over to Gainesville and the University of Florida, she chanced to meet a doctoral student by the name of Archie Carr. It was love at first sight and after a brief engagement Marjorie and Archie married in January, 1937. In the early years the couple occasionally visited Marjorie's family in Bonita Springs and were regular visitors to the Reptile Gardens. They were always happy to see the Pipers and to marvel at how the collection had grown. Lester Piper was very proud that Archie Carr had given him an autographed copy of his monograph, *A Contribution to the Herpetology of Florida* that was published in 1940.

Archie Carr went on in life to become the premier sea turtle specialist of the twentieth century, and because of his research and conservation efforts, he is widely known as the "man who saved sea turtles." Two of his popular commercial books, *The Windward Road*, and *So Excellent a Fishe*, are among the greatest reads of the twentieth century. Marjorie Carr raised five children and was active in environmental movements. In her own right, she was dubbed, "the woman who killed the Cross-Florida Barge Canal." This was a grand milestone achievement in environmental activism. Completion of this ill-advised project was stopped dead in its tracks by Marjorie's efforts in 1971, when President Richard Nixon signed an executive order that halted the ugly ditch's construction.

Executives from the National Audubon Society in New York City became frequent visitors to the Gardens in the mid-1950s to consult with Bill Piper, after the organization finally initiated an effort to save the Corkscrew Swamp and its wood stork rookery in Collier County. Bill had taken a speciaal interest in seeing this national treasure preserved, in 1954. He had become personally dedicated and vocally active in doing his part in protecting the wild and unspoiled Corkscrew Swamp. He worked closely with the Audubon Society to keep that pristine cypress forest from being destroyed by loggers. Bill Piper raised many thousands of dollars for the acquisition of the Corkscrew Swamp.

Directors of the nation's major zoological parks and natural history museums frequently visited the Pipers, and were at first astonished at the wildlife diversity on display, and then on repeat visits always thrilled to see the exhibit. All were amazed at the variety of wildlife and the excellent health of the captives that were housed in the Piper collection. All of them were awed by the size of the specimens and the overall size of the collection of American crocodiles. Many visiting zookeepers tried to talk Bill and Lester into parting with some of the giants, but to no avail. Occasionally, a smaller crocodile might be "loaned" out, but that was a rarity.

Marlin Perkins, Director of the Lincoln Park Zoo in Chicago, and James Oliver, Curator of Reptiles at the famous Bronx Zoo, in New York, always visited the Pipers when they were in the area. Bill Piper occasionally took them on snake-collecting trips out into the Big Cypress Swamp. Lester spent time with these men discussing the husbandry of wild animals. After Lester had loaned James Oliver a small American crocodile, the curator returned the favor and shipped Lester a West African dwarf crocodile and a young Nile crocodile. I suspect that many years later, after it had grown to impressive proportions, that this very Nile crocodile was the crocodile that replaced "Big Joe" after the American crocodile of that name died. The original Big Joe was toothless[67] and was displayed alone, kept in solitary confinement for years, because of his belligerence with other crocodiles in the big pen. Newspaper accounts reported that Big Joe died on April 29, 2003, so it isn't possible to determine the crocodile's true identity as to species, unless the animal's skull was saved.

The Wonder Gardens always received good press. Whenever unusual animals were added to the collection, or captive-born or rehabilitated animals released, the Fort Myers and Naples newspapers gave the events great coverage. Activity and social columns in the papers usually announced when school groups had visited and reported on the educational benefits the students had derived from the visits. Major national magazines ran feature stories about the Piper brothers and their Gardens. Among them were the Saturday Evening Post, Look Magazine, Collier's Weekly, and True Magazine.

Ralph Curtis remembers when the Governor of Kentucky and his family visited, and Lester asked him to give the governor's party a private tour. Later, Ralph guided actress Gloria Swanson, who wintered in Naples, Florida, around the Gardens. When Arthur Fiedler and the entire Boston Pops Orchestra visited the Gardens, Ralph was also called on to conduct a special tour. As *Wind Across the Everglades* was being filmed in Everglades City, I gave tours to Burl Ives, Christopher Plummer, Peter Falk, and Gypsy Rose Lee. In 1958, I gave a special private tour for August A. Busch, Jr., — like in the Anheuser-Busch brewery empire — and his entourage. He was visiting all zoos and wildlife exhibits in Florida to get an idea of what kind of wild animal attractions already existed, scoping out the competition as he began to develop plans for his grandiose wild animal attraction — Busch Gardens, in Tampa.

A tiny minority of the people who visited the Gardens was unhappy with their experience. Some couldn't get beyond the nasty odor of the sulfur water, and others were emotionally vocal about the small quarters delegated to the animals on exhibit. The odor of the water was beyond the control of man, much less the Piper brothers. The quartering of animals, in what were perceived by some as tiny cages, was not unlike the practice of most of the large metropolitan zoological parks during the period. It was long after the Bonita Springs Reptile Gardens were up and running that a trend for large habitat displays came into vogue at the large zoos, and by then it was too late for the Piper's to implement such exhibits. They simply didn't have the room. Caged large mammals like the Florida panthers, Florida black bears, and Florida bobcats, periodically paced back and forth in the front of their cages for exercise. This activity may have inaccurately conveyed to some visitors that the captives suffered from a level of boredom or unhappiness, but in reality there were no other captive animals on the planet that were better cared for. A demanding Lester Piper insured that was the case — because the man literally loved each and every one of his animals.

Lester raised domestic pork for his dinner table on the Garden's grounds. A large pen that was located on the north end of the property, between Bill's residence and the Wonder Gardens Restaurant, at any one time held about a dozen pigs. Their feed, mostly scraps obtained from area restaurants and markets, was cooked in a large slop barrel nearby. Periodically, the fire would have to be lit to cook the swill. We always used lighter pine to stoke the fire after shoving some newspaper under it to get it started.

Frank Liles was a fifteen-year-old Bonita Springs teenager who worked part-time at the Gardens. This particular day he was sent to relight the hog pot fire. After he prepared everything, Frank fetched a coffee can full of gasoline to toss on the wood after he'd lit the paper. As he swung his arm to cast the gasoline, some of it spilled and soaked his pants leg. In a split-second the fire flashed back and Frank was ablaze. At this instant, I happened to be walking under the pole shed nearby as Frank ran toward me in flames. I responded by tackling him and rolling him over and over on the sandy ground, sweeping handfuls of the sand on his jeans to extinguish the flames. I soon had the fire smothered without any serious burns to either of us. Many years later, Lester moved his hog pen to *his* Bonita Springs Pasture.

Frequently, wild animal dealers visited the Gardens to see if Lester was in the market for some unusual critter or to deliver specimens that Lester had ordered. One of these was Brad Bradford. Brad routinely visited to see if he had any creatures aboard his truck that would interest Lester. The truck was a huge military surplus vehicle with a canvas-covered bed. The bed contained a topsy-turvy tiered arrangement of cages, which usually held a variety of wild animals that Bradford offered for sale.

Within a couple of years after Ralph Curtis left Lester's employ, in late 1953, he went to work for Tarpon Zoo, a wildlife exhibit and wild animal dealership on U.S. 19 near Tarpon Springs, Florida. The owners wanted to expand to the Florida east coast where most of the wildlife importers were based. Ralph relocated to Hollywood, Florida, and opened "Wild Cargo" as a subsidiary of Tarpon Zoo. He would frequently return to Bonita Springs to deliver animals that Lester ordered on a regular basis, like roseate spoonbills, scarlet ibis, wood storks, king vultures, black-necked stilts, and crested caracaras — species that could legally be imported and sold during that time.

In 1969, the Florida Game and Freshwater Fish Commission amended the Florida Wildlife Code and added a new section pertaining to the proper care of captive wildlife within the state. This new section regulated and provided guidelines for the correct care and housing of native wildlife species as promulgated by Commission biologists and their allied experts. All wildlife exhibits, zoological parks, and wildlife specimens in the custody of private collectors, were subject to the new requirements. The Florida Game and Freshwater Fish Commission began regularly inspecting captive wildlife facilities in 1970.

Lieutenant Barry Cook was appointed Wildlife Inspector for the section of peninsular Florida that is situated between Hernando and Collier Counties. Everglades Wonder Gardens fell under his jurisdiction. Barry made his first inspection visit there early in 1973. This was after Lester Piper had received copies of all the new requirements and had enough advance notice and sufficient time to at least begin bringing everything up to the new standards stipulated under the revised wildlife code.

Lieutenant Cook introduced himself at the Wonder Gardens entrance to Lucille Piper and he was granted entry to conduct his inspection. Lester was busy preparing the evening feed for his charges and would meet Cook in the slaughterhouse when he had completed his walk through. The officer carefully noted the infractions he observed and as he interpreted them. The actual field reports are no longer available for this inspection because the agency, now the Florida Fish and Wildlife Conservation Commission, has had a long-standing policy that after twenty years such papers are destroyed, and not archived. Now, thirty-six years later, there is no paper trail that will indicate what problems were noted and brought to Lester Piper's attention during that first inspection.

Barry Cook verbally reviewed his inspection, item by item, one on one with Lester while the two men stood on opposite sides of the butcher table. Lester was now seventy-one years of age, with a steadily worsening hearing handicap. He simply couldn't hear all of Barry's words and because of that he didn't comprehend everything that officer Cook was telling him. Lester couldn't understand why the Game Commission was suddenly pushing him around. After all, he and Bill had been good friends of the agency, working closely with the leadership and most of their biologists and law enforcement officers over the years. His own opinion of the agency had spoiled after one of the panthers he had loaned to the Game Commission had to be put down after it had been injured while in their care. Despite his own views, Lester always thought that his and Bill's relationship with Tallahassee was on an even keel. Lester became utterly confused, and then belligerent. He stopped cutting up the pile of boned meat he was slicing into large cubes, and was now talking louder, so he could hear himself. As he spoke Lester became more irritated and began gesturing; without thinking about the fact that he was waving his butcher knife wildly around over the table. Blunt as always, Lester informed officer Cook, "I've forgotten more about how to take care of wild animals than you or the rest of the wonder boys in your outfit will ever know!" Barry Cook looked at the moving knife in the hand of the irate man across the table, and took a deep breath. He was young and somewhat inexperienced when it came to dealing with an angry and argumentative old man the likes of Lester Piper, and this was a real test of his training. Barry called on his communication skills and he managed to diplomatically defuse the situation. Lester finally started to calm down. Over time, during future annual inspections, the two men tolerated one another and Lester moved to positively conform to the new mandates — slowly, because he never agreed with them. Until the end, he thought amateurs were shoving stupid rules down his throat.

In 1983, Warren Boutchia, Ralph Curtis, George Weymouth and I got together after deciding we all wanted to take a ride down to Bonita Springs and visit Lester — a genuine trip down Memory Lane. All of us, except Warren, were living on Sanibel Island, and he had driven down from his home outside of Tampa. None of us had seen Lester in a few years, and he was genuinely happy to see all of us. We found him in good health and spirits, and although we noticed he had slowed down just a little, the five of us walked around the Gardens looking at the wildlife and telling stories about the old days. When we were finished, we left the yard and dodged his mean guard dog, which was chained near the gate to slow down any non-employees who might want to stroll through, and we all went into the slaughterhouse. We continued joking and laughing, again talking about old times, Lester's old buddies who were characters we had all known, and some of the people we had all worked with and were also gone.

Those of us who helped butcher cattle, horses, or mules in this room all remembered and told a similar tale of how Lester trained us. The dead animal that was to be rendered into animal food was lowered with a chain-hoist onto its back to rest on a cradle dolly. Lester would then make a long incision along the bottom of its abdomen and he and a couple of us would begin skinning the animal. The hide would be cut into smaller pieces as it was removed and tossed into a bucket. These chunks would later go to the mid-sized alligators and crocodiles. After all of the hide was off that we could reach and that was not in contact with the dolly, Lester would expand the belly incision deeper into the body cavity to expose the intestines, prior to hoisting the animal up for gutting and quartering. If he were training a novice, watch out. I remember when he pulled this on Richard Beatty. With an astonished tone in his voice, he said, "What the hell is that?" Richard replied, "What?"

After that, Lester continued pointing, and said, "That little thing right there." Richard bent over and kept getting closer and closer, trying to see what Lester was talking about and pointing at. When his face was just inches away, Lester jabbed a hole in the animal's digestive tract and the rushing gas that had been trapped inside exploded into Richard's face, instantly nauseating him. I thought he was going to pass out. Lester then became hysterical, and with a roar of laughter, he danced around, totally happy that someone else had been victimized by his ploy. He had once done the same thing to me. It wasn't as funny as he thought it was. Someone added the story of how Lester would also slip an empty beer or soft drink can into an animal's gut for one of the new workers to discover and become at least perplexed by for a few moments, as they wondered, "How in the hell did that get in there?"

Photo from the author's collection.

Left to right, George Weymouth, Charles LeBuff, Lester Piper, Ralph Curtis, and Warren Boutchia at Lester's pasture, in 1983. Lester's grandson, Lester "Bucky" W. Piper, took this photo for us.

Our visit was winding down when all of a sudden, Lester asked, "Do you want to see my cows?" We all said, "Sure," and the five of us went out and jumped in his pickup truck; two in the cab with him and two in the bed, and off we went. We were headed for the former Piper brothers' Bonita Springs pasture, that since the dissolution of his partnership with Bill was now Lester's personal pasture. Lester was proud that he owned his own small herd of cattle, and he drove us through his pasture as he inspected them. It had been a great day for us all.

As the collection of wildlife and the responsibility of their care grew, Lester himself seldom ventured out into the outside world beyond the Everglades Wonder Gardens gate. Once a year he would shed his work clothes, dress up, and attend the annual meetings of the Florida Attractions Association. He and Lucille would occasionally leave the premises to go out to dinner. Otherwise, his trips outside the Everglades Wonder Gardens compound were confined to picking up animals or meat scraps and produce from area stores, and for the rare personal medically related appointment.

In 1960, he left long enough to make a couple of trips to Sanibel Island. I was helping to set up a wildlife conservation themed exhibit for the Sanibel-Captiva Audubon Society in which I was active. They traditionally had a table and exhibits at the annual Sanibel Shell Fair. I came up with the idea to exhibit an eagle and the only captive eagles I knew about close by were the two at Everglades Wonder Gardens. I really doubted that I could pull it off, but I was committed to try. So, I called Lester and asked if he would loan me an eagle. He thought it over for a few minutes, and after I pledged that I would personally care for the bird, he agreed. He would put the bird in a small display cage and he would also supply all the food it would need during its visit. When I tried to set a day and time for me to drive to Bonita Springs, he interrupted me, "No, I'll bring it up to you on the morning the Shell Fair starts. I haven't been up to Sanibel for a while. Last time I was there was to catch a gator in the boat basin between the ferry landing and the lighthouse. I believe he had killed your boss' dog[68]." I was completely surprised when he told me he would actually take the time to come to the island. Lester followed through and even returned on Sunday to pick the bird up. Thanks to Lester Piper, the bald eagle made our Audubon Society's table a huge success.

Chapter 27

The Final Division

ON SEPTEMBER 1, 1966, Lester's son David was sent to Bill's home to check on his aunt, Alida Piper. She had been discharged from the state hospital and returned to Bonita Springs in 1958. Alida had seemed moody for a couple of days, and Bill had stopped by on his way out to the pasture that morning and asked Lester to have someone check in on his wife later in the day. Alida was the organist at The Saint Leo's Catholic Church in Bonita Springs, and according to David Piper she practiced every day. Her often-loud music was regularly heard throughout the Gardens and around the neighborhood. David remembered that the more alcohol Alida consumed, the louder her music became. The organ was noticeably silent on this particular day, and Lester noticed the quiet and decided to send David over to check on Alida. The specific time of day that David banged on the door is unclear. He could not raise a response, so he went inside the house to investigate and found Alida's nude body on the bedroom floor. From all appearances she had been dead for several hours. Memories are vague as to what happened after David reported his horrid discovery to Lester. Anecdotal commentary suggests that someone went out to the pasture to give Bill the grizzly news. Bill returned home immediately, and according to newspaper accounts, he called and notified the Lee County Sheriff's Department at 5:11 p.m. Lee County deputies and investigators were dispatched to the Piper home where they found a .22 caliber pistol beside the body. Their investigation found no evidence of foul play. Alida's death was ruled a suicide[69] by Lee County Judge Thomas W. Shands.

Bill threw himself into his work after Alida's death and his involvement in the operation of the Gardens was further reduced. He rekindled his interest in the cattle business, making an effort to put this tragedy behind him and move on. He entered a new relationship and married a local woman about four years after Alida's death.

Bill Piper married Myrtle "Emie" Irene Hodges on September 2, 1970. Emie Piper's new in-laws, Lester and Lucille Piper, were not thrilled when Bill remarried. Emie Piper had grown up in Bonita Springs. In the fifties she and my wife, the former Jean Williams[70], were very close friends. Emie had three sons during a previous relationship and Bill later adopted her children. Emie bore Bill his first and only child, Anna May Piper, who they named after his mother.

After Bill remarried, Lester began to intensify his effort to get Bill to agree to end the Piper brothers' partnership and divide their assets equally. This had been discussed between the two brothers for several years, originating back to about the time Bill had expanded into the cattle business, but the subject was never brought anywhere close to a point of finalization. Lester saw conflict ahead, convinced that legal wrangling between survivors would be a certainty when one of the brothers died. Even with both brothers living, there was already argument and conflict because of the indecision to legally end the partnership and divide things up between them. Bill continually dragged his feet on the issue while Lester thought it imperative that they end their partnership to avoid major problems and legal wrangling between their survivors if either he or Bill should suddenly die. Remember, their partnership agreement had been verbal, between two brothers, with nothing ever put down on paper. In the opinion of Lester's legal counsel, it was a catastrophe waiting to happen, and Lester Piper was advised that was the case. The heated brotherly debates became more frequent as time dragged on. Finally, after all the procrastination by Bill, their attorneys managed to work out a formula that was amenable to them both for fair distribution of the partnership's assets. During the negotiations, it was agreed that Bill would retain title to lots 1 and 4 of Block B of Spring Gardens subdivision[71]. These were the lots at Everglades Wonder Gardens where his residence was situated. Bill had already vacated the home after building a new residence near the Palm River Subdivision in Collier County, but he wanted to retain title to the house and lots at Everglades Wonder Gardens.

They executed a document on December 31, 1981, that was titled "Agreement to Wind Up Partnership Everglades Wonder Gardens." The key elements of this agreement were:

1.   The partners are parties to an oral partnership known as EVERGLADES WONDER GARDENS, located in Bonita Springs, Florida, which was established in **1938** and has as its activities ranching, a gift shop and an animal exhibit.

2.   The partners desire to dissolve the partnership and distribute the assets thereof.

Noteworthy is the stipulated date of origin of the Piper partnership — **1938** — in Section 1 of the above Agreement. This suggests that in the very beginning of Bonita Springs Reptile Gardens both brothers weren't on board and there was no partnership. The year also corroborates what I was told by Alfred Trew; that Lester arrived in Bonita Springs to stay and became personally involved in the project after Bill had started developing the Bonita Springs Reptile Gardens.

The document stipulated that the partnership would be dissolved on December 31, 1981, and it authorized that Lester could continue to use the name "Everglades Wonder Gardens." There was another document associated with the above Agreement titled, "NOTICE OF DISSOLUTION OF PARTNERSHIP AND CONTINUATION OF BUSINESS." This was also dated December 31, 1981, and states:

TO WHOM IT MAY CONCERN:

Notice is hereby given that the partnership known as EVERGLADES WONDER GARDENS, PIPER AND PIPER, located in Bonita Springs, Florida, shall be dissolved as of December 31, 1981.

WILFORD J. PIPER and LESTER T. PIPER hereby certify that WILFORD J. PIPER has withdrawn from said partnership this 31 day of December, 1981, and has assigned his interest therein to LESTER T. PIPER, together with the right to continue such business under the name of EVERGLADES WONDER GARDENS.

A "Certificate of Valuation" was attached to the above-cited Agreement. This document tagged the value of the partnership's assets. Each brother accepted and signed off on this document.

So, after years of bickering with his older brother, Lester Piper finally got the Everglades Wonder Gardens real estate, exclusive of the two lots of Bill's home site, the business and the wildlife livestock, after paying Bill a dollar amount equal to the value of fifty percent of the wildlife collection, the 167.55-acre Bonita Springs pasture, and a section of the Mule Pens pasture property that was included in a mining lease with another party. Bill would get the remaining sections of land at Mule Pens. Lester also agreed to Bill's demand that Bill's name would be removed from all advertising pertaining to Everglades Wonder Gardens.

During a conversation with me in 2005, Bill's widow, Emie, told me, "I had to take Bill all over the state, to every wild animal dealer, exhibit, and zoo he could think of so he could figure out what the wild animal inventory at the Wonder Gardens was worth. After all that, he figured his share to be $25,000.00, and that's what he got from Lester for all the animals[72]."

Chapter 28

When All Was Said and Done

BILL AND LESTER PIPER were together on February 22, 1986, for what was considered to be the fiftieth anniversary of Everglades Wonder Gardens. They were surrounded by some of their oldest friends from the Bonita Springs and Lee County communities, and many former employees were on hand to help celebrate. It was a fun evening, and I managed to capture much of it on videotape.

The Piper brothers aged reasonably well. The last time that I saw and spoke to them was at this anniversary party for Everglades Wonder Gardens. Lester's hearing had continued to fail, and he half-heartedly wore a hearing aid. He had been a thirty-year survivor of cancer after a bout with throat cancer in the mid-fifties. Although eighty-six-years old at the time, Bill seemed to have aged the more gracefully of the two brothers.

Over the next three years following this celebration, Bill's health continued to decline, and worsened after he made an unannounced visit to the Wonder Gardens in February, 1988, while he was still mobile and able to drive himself around. It was after closing time, and Bill wanted to drop in and visit Lester. He opened a gate, casually walked through, and was unexpectedly confronted by one of Lester's ill-tempered guard dogs. The dog did not recognize Bill, and having no respect for his advanced age, it immediately attacked him. The powerful animal charged and knocked Bill down and he fell hard on the concrete walkway. Covering his face with his hands, he tried to ward off the dog's vicious attack. Bill was severely mauled by the dog. He was bitten on the head, his hands, and his arms multiple times, and he was badly banged and scraped up from falling on the concrete before Lester heard the commotion outside his kitchen and realized what was going on. He got outside as quickly as he could and got the dog under control and off of his brother. Bill had to be hospitalized for several days, and according to his daughter Anna, "My dad was never the same after that dog attacked him. That's when he started to go downhill fast." Lester offered to have the dog put down, but Bill insisted otherwise, telling him, "No, he was just doing his job."

Lester (Left) and Bill Piper, 1986, at the fiftieth anniversary party celebrating their creation, Everglades Wonder Gardens.

Not long before Bill passed away, Lester received a telephone call that his brother was bedridden, was slipping away, and didn't have too much time left. Lester told his son, David, "I want to go see my brother." David drove his father down to Bill's home and the Piper brothers visited for the last time and said their goodbyes to one another. Soon after that farewell visit, it was Bill Piper who left us first. He died at home, on January 13, 1989, a week after his eighty-ninth birthday. Bill had once told his nephew, David, that upon his death he wanted his body to be donated to the University of Florida School of Medicine for medical research purposes. Ultimately, he was cremated and his family spread his remains on the water he loved near Bonita Springs. His wife Emie Piper passed away on July 20, 2007. At this writing, Bill and Emie Piper have three grandchildren.

Author Bill Snyder best described Bill Piper when he summed the man up in one sentence, "The Everglades was his classroom and Mother Nature his only teacher, but Bill Piper's homespun knowledge of wildlife has earned the envy of many a professional biologist." What more can I add to that?

Lester Piper carried on and continued his daily routine in the operation of Everglades Wonder Gardens until the very end. That came soon after he was diagnosed with an aneurism in his chest. Ken Morrison tried to discourage Lester from having the corrective surgery that the specialist in Naples was recommending. Ken told Lester, "If that thing explodes you'll probably die in less than a minute, but if they screw up, it'll probably take you a while to die. If they don't do anything at all about it, it may never bust and you'll live for a few more years, and something else will end up killing you."

The surgeon had convinced Lester that the risk was low, and he decided to go ahead and have the operation. Lester was admitted to Naples Community Hospital for corrective surgery, but he did not survive the procedure and died on April 25, 1992. His wife Lucille passed away on October 22, 1993. They are buried in Naples Memorial Gardens, just a few miles south of Bonita Springs. Lester and Lucille Piper have four grandchildren, eleven great-grandchildren, and five great-great grandchildren (and one on the way, at this writing) surviving.

Eighty-seven year old Lester Piper is still in charge, giving orders, and sweating with the crew, in 1989.

I'll always remember Lester Piper's sage advice, often uttered with a Shakespearean twinkle in his eyes. These were the words that he probably uttered to everyone that ever worked for him or had grown close to him at one time or another. His voice still sounds in my head, "The world's not your oyster."

Epilogue

IT HAS BEEN MY complete pleasure and honor to present this definitive work on the lives of Wilford and Lester Piper, the founders of Everglades Wonder Gardens. In today's world of grand-scale eco-tourism, expensive well-staffed publicly and privately funded visitor centers have replaced Florida's nearly extinct roadside zoos and wildlife attractions. It must not be discounted; these disappearing tourist attractions once filled a special niche and educated people by the thousands during the last century.

As I write the final words and complete this biography, Everglades Wonder Gardens has been open to the public for seventy-four years. This Florida attraction was once the premier wildlife-oriented tourist destination in Florida. Today, the land and business are owned by two of Lester Piper's grandsons — David T. Piper, Jr. and Lester W. Piper. After the death of his mother, David T. Piper, Sr. transferred ownership of Everglades Wonder Gardens to his oldest sons on April 30, 1997. The former of the two men is the operator of Everglades Wonder Gardens. He has often publicly stated that it is his paramount goal to continue to honor the wildlife work of his late grandfather. David even went the extra mile and had Lester Piper's portrait tattooed on one of his forearms to convey his affection for his late grandfather. David Piper, Jr. has struggled, and done well, to keep what he interprets as Lester Piper's dream afloat. But, his interpretation excludes much of that dream's foundation that was originally based on the genius of Lester Piper's brother, Bill.

Since Lester's death in 1992, the character of the Everglades Wonder Gardens operation has been beset by adversarial changes demanded by state and federal regulatory agencies — edicts from the very wonder boys Lester Piper disliked. The long-standing permits held by Lester Piper that were applicable to Everglades Wonder Gardens expired at the time of his death, and it became a whole new ball game for the younger Pipers. In many cases, cage sizes and wet/dry percentages of wet enclosures had to be modified to conform to the rules imposed by state and federal bureaucracies, and the Gardens of today are not those exactly envisioned and nurtured for so long by Lester Piper. Were Lester confronted with these issues as a younger man, he would have worked diligently toward compliance with the new rules. No one person is to blame. The changes have been created because of public policies and modern perceptions about caged wildlife, so the small independent roadside zoos are no longer part of the Florida mystique that once attracted tourists to these facilities by the thousands.

It is inevitable. We are approaching the time when this chapter in Florida's early history will close, and the era of small privately-owned wildlife exhibits will end, but first I will take this opportunity to challenge David Piper, Jr. and Lester W. Piper to honor both their grandfather and their grand uncle in a meaningful and lasting way. When the doors of Everglades Wonder Gardens are closed forever, these men need to step forward and walk the walk; there will not be any time left for just talking the talk. They should walk up to the plate and deed a small piece of the Everglades Wonder Gardens property, a tiny parcel of Lot 6, of Block C, in the Spring Gardens Subdivision — the corner bordered by the old Tamiami Trail and the Imperial River — to the City of Bonita Springs as a mini-park. That is, after they negotiate an agreement with the city that stipulates that this parcel is to be used exclusively for one purpose, for the location of a site to erect a monument to honor the lives of the Piper brothers, in recognition of their lifetime contributions to Bonita Springs, and their generous gift of free entry to the Gardens to her citizens during their long lifetimes — and establish this memorial in perpetuity.

Wilford James Piper died January 13, 1989, in North Naples, Collier County, Florida.

Lester Thomas Piper died April 25, 1992, in Naples, Collier County, Florida.

NOTES

Chapter 1   *Dangerous Times*

1 Another name for a speakeasy, a place where alcoholic drinks were sold illegally during Prohibition.
2 From 2009 interviews with Alfred Trew, and Anna Piper Mackereth.

Chapter 2   *Family Roots*

3 Although I requested documentation from the Lancaster Fire Department, I have been unsuccessful in locating and obtaining a roster or a service record that provides the actual dates of his employment with that fire department.
4 In an Affidavit executed on May 16, 1955, and filed at the Lee County Courthouse, Bill corrects his name because it was erroneously spelled "Wilfred" on a deed. He affirmed that his name was Wilford J. Piper.

Chapter 3   *Growing Up*

5 Bill would later reach a high level of education because he later advanced to a responsible rank in the U.S. Navy.

Chapter 4   *Anchors Aweigh*

6 Today the United States Navy Reserve.
7 The information in this chapter regarding Bill Piper's time in the U.S. Navy is based on his official file that I obtained from the National Personnel Records Center, of the National Archives and Records Administration, via Request Number 1-6683128040.
8 The U.S. Naval Air Station at Moutchic, France, was one of the largest U.S. Navy training centers in Europe.
9 Lighter-than-air-craft; i.e., dirigibles.
10 This certificate is in the custody of Anna Piper Mackereth.
11 An enlisted sailor who is responsible for steering a ship and its navigation during his (or her) watch and the maintenance, upgrading, and preparation of nautical charts and navigation publications holds the rank of Quartermaster aboard a U.S. Navy ship.

Chapter 5   *Life on the River*

12 By this time Bill and Frances Piper had relocated to the Ocala, Florida, area.
13 The crew was armed because there was a constant threat that rival bootleggers would try to highjack loads of alcohol.

14 *From Booze, Boats & Bad Times*, George Gouth, 2004, p. 34.

Chapter 6   *Finding a Place to Roost*

15 This ledger is among the papers currently in the custody of Anna Piper Mackereth.

16 This ledger is titled "Reptile Farm" and the first entry is dated April 21, 1934.

17 The prices they paid for "baby" alligators averaged $.25 each.

18 A religious utopian sect based in Estero, Florida, publisher of the "American Eagle."

19 Bonita Springs was first incorporated in 1925.

Chapter 7   *In the Beginning*

20 Water temperature in degrees Fahrenheit.

21 Now the independent nation of Belize.

22 Bill had flown in dirigibles previously, while in the Navy. His brother Lester never flew in an aircraft.

23 *Adventures With Reptiles: The Story of Ross Allen*, C.J. Hylander, 1951, p.125.

24 After the death of Lester Piper, representatives of a Native American group visited the Gardens and demanded these artifacts be turned over to them. According to David Piper, Sr., they were.

25 The date of opening was published as being February 22, 1936, in a Naples newspaper account about Everglades Wonder Gardens. I have been unable to independently verify that this date is accurate for the beginning of the Piper operation in Bonita Springs. It is possible this date is based on when Bill Piper made the decision to go into the wild animal business in Marion County with Ross Allen, and 1937 seems a more precise year for the development of the Bonita Springs Reptile Gardens to have started. Since the Pipers obtained their first Occupational Licenses for the operation in 1938, it makes that year more realistic.

Chapter 9   *Stars of the Show*

26 These are dermal pressure receptors. In the case of alligators they are a series of tiny pit-like sensors arranged along their jaws.

27 *The Alligator Snapping Turtle*, P.C.H. Pritchard, (Revised Edition) 2006, p. 49. In addition, page 50 contains a photograph of Bill Piper holding one of his and Lester's near record skulls of this species.

28 Surgery to permanently disable a bird by surgically removing the wing at the pinion joint. In this case, one wing.

Chapter 11   *The Crocodile Kings*

29 Bob Halgrim attended the Gardens' 50th anniversary party, in 1986.
30 Lester Piper would roll over in his grave if he knew that The Shell Factory that was founded by his old commercial nemesis, Harold Crant, continues to host a popular Wildlife Park, in 2010.
31 This is the second fictitious name the Pipers used for their attraction.
32 The Miami Serpentarium founder, Bill Haast, closed his attraction and retired in 1984. At the time of writing he is still living, and keeps venomous snakes, near Punta Gorda, in Charlotte County.
33 Now known as The Naples Zoo at Caribbean Gardens.

Chapter 12   *The Movies*

34 Later Luby became my sister Natalie Kirkland's, father-in-law.

Chapter 13   *When Panthers Ruled*

35 Many years later he would accept a cast-off African lion, a jaguar, and even monkeys and add them to the collection.
36 Images of all three items may be found on the Everglades Wonder Gardens' web site linked to www.sanybel.com.
37 *The Florida Panther*, D.S. Maeher, 1997, p. 169.
38 This is a factual statement. The Florida panthers at Everglades Wonder Gardens were all descendants of wild caught specimens. The "characteristics" of Florida panthers mentioned by Baudy are folly-based.
39 This letter is still among Bill Piper's papers.

Chapter 14   *Old Slewfoot's Retirement Years*

40 Quoted from "The Man Who Grows His Own Wildlife", a feature article written by Bill Snyder that appeared in an unknown magazine, date unknown (but likely in the very early 1950s).
41 Occasionally this diet was supplemented with the addition of fish, like filets of jack cravelle.
42 This is not the smaller cage in which Tom was taken to the Naples Drive-In Theater.
43 *Naples' Oldest Tradition Swamp Buggy Days*, L. Zuch, 2009, pp. 48, 69, and 200.
44 Italics are mine.

Chapter 16   *Guitars and Gators Don't Mix*

45 Bearing eggs, as opposed to being pregnant and giving live birth.
46 In 1977, a six-year old boy fell into the crocodile pit at the Miami Serpentarium and was killed by the lone American crocodile in the pit.

Chapter 17   *Bill Piper's Déjà Vu*

47 This date is based on a personnel spreadsheet, provided to me by the Florida Fish and Wildlife Conservation Commission.
48 From The Collier County News issue of Friday, June 17, 1955.
49 In 2005, the Maxcy family sold off a huge parcel of this ranchland, 27,400 acres, for $137 million.

Chapter 18   *Scaled Danger*

50 The same building that once housed the Baird's Camp Tavern.

Chapter 20   *Tragedy Strikes Again*

51 Much of the information in this chapter is based on newspaper accounts and a Florida Supreme Court document from a 1989 appeal hearing.
52 On December 22, 1954.

Chapter 21   *Snake Hunting With Lester Piper*

53 Even submerged cars from the forties with human remains in them have been discovered during canal maintenance in recent years.
54 Where the entrance of Collier-Seminole State Park is located.
55 Formerly known as red-bellied mud snakes.
56 Formerly known Allen's or striped swamp snake.
57 In 1958, I collected a five-foot, four-inch female cottonmouth from underneath one of these culverts between Naples and Royal Palm Hammock. It lived at Everglades Wonder Gardens for years thereafter.
58 Now the relocated Miami/Dade Metro Zoo.

Chapter 22   *The Buck Shack*

59 Lester Piper and Ken Morrison gave it this name.

Chapter 23   *Lester, the Intimidator*

60 During interviews one individual told me this happened at The Dome, while another claimed it happened at a small juke joint with a forgotten name on the west side of the Trail between the Gardens and The Shell Factory. David Piper, Sr. remembers that it happened at Baird's.

61 Bill was selling cows all along, but he may not have told his brother. A note in his cattle ledger states that on March 24, 1980, he sold twenty-eight head, and reaped $8,748.38.

62 Today, these U.S. Fish and Wildlife Service law enforcement officers are known as Special Agents.

63 When Lester wanted another eagle, and with bald eagles out of the question, I found a wild animal dealer in Montana that offered golden eagles at $60.00 each. Lester bought two.

Chapter 24   *Jones Comes "Jonesing" For Dough*

64 Arthur Jones' centerfold-candidate trophy spouse at the time. Jones was famous for his oft-repeated motto, "Bigger crocodiles, faster airplanes, and younger women!"

65 A former linebacker for the Chicago Bears. In 1979 he was inducted into the Professional Football Hall of Fame.

66 Arthur Jones had invented this exercise apparatus, founded Nautilus, and became a multimillionaire.

Chapter 26   *Visitors at the Gate*

67 This adult male American crocodile was very aggressive, and through the years he completely lost his teeth in fights or biting or striking his enclosure with his head. Crocodiles can regrow their teeth, but in the case of Big Joe, the supply of substitute teeth must have become exhausted.

68 A ten-foot alligator killed the dog of W.D. "Tommy" Wood in the old "Kinzie Yacht Basin" just west of the Sanibel Island Lighthouse, circa 1951.

Chapter 27   *The Final Division*

69 From a page 3-A story, "Mrs. Bill Piper Shoots Self," in the Fort-Myers News-Press, dated September 3, 1966.

70 The Williams family arrived in Bonita Springs in 1918.

71 Lester and Lucille Piper had released their share of the two lots to Bill on April 29, 1959.

72 In comparison, the value of the livestock on the ranch was established at $85,000.00.

ROSS ALLEN'S REPTILE INSTITUTE

SILVER SPRINGS, FLORIDA

REGULAR PRICE LIST
1939

E. ROSS ALLEN

CORAL SNAKE

PHONE 1000 BLACK
TELEGRAPH VIA OCALA, FLA.
CABLE FLAREP

SNAKES
ALLIGATORS
CROCODILES
TURTLES
LIZARDS
SNAKE VENOM
PRESERVED REPTILES
MERCHANDISE

**Good Specimens with Prompt Service
for Reasonable Prices**

Copyright, E. Ross Allen, January, 1939

After the end of his business relationship with Bill Piper, Ross Allen went on and expanded the scope of his Reptile Institute. This is one of his earliest price lists.

Index

Charles LeBuff on the Sanibel Island beach, at the helm of Caretta Research, Inc.. He pioneered sea turtle conservation in southwest Florida.

A Note About the Author

CHARLES LeBUFF WAS BORN in Massachusetts. He moved to Bonita Springs, Florida with his parents and three siblings, in 1952. In 1953, Charles became an interpretive naturalist — a guide at Bill and Lester Piper's Everglades Wonder Gardens. He remained there, with the exception of an eight-month absence, until the end of 1958 when he was selected for a position on Sanibel Island, Florida, with the U.S. Fish and Wildlife Service. He had left the Gardens in 1957 to take an earlier position with the federal agency in Naples, at their Red Tide Field Station, but when the laboratory was to be relocated to Saint Petersburg Beach he decided to stay put in southwest Florida. In early 1958 Charles returned to work at Everglades Wonder Gardens for another year while waiting to receive the appointment to the position he had been selected to fill by the U.S. Fish and Wildlife Service on Sanibel Island.

He spent thirty-two years at J.N. "Ding" Darling National Wildlife Refuge and he retired in 1990, but remained on the island until 2005. During his time on Sanibel Island, and in other than his official capacity, he served as president of the Sanibel-Captiva Audubon Society, was a founding board member of the Sanibel-Captiva Conservation Foundation, was twice elected to the Sanibel City Council, serving his community from 1974 to 1980, and he founded and directed the loggerhead turtle conservation project, Caretta Research, Inc. Today, he and his wife Jean, a Bonita Springs native, live in Fort Myers, Florida, where he writes, carves wood, and is learning to master the acoustic guitar.